P9-APF-564

Arms Control and
International Security

Also of Interest

†Available in hardcover and paperback.

Westview Special Studies in International Relations

Arms Control and International Security
edited by Roman Kolkowicz and Neil Joeck

Designed to introduce the reader to the critical issues of arms control and international security in the 1980s, this collection of provocative and challenging articles encourages a rethinking of conventional wisdom on strategic policy. The authors succinctly convey the tensions existing between those who would eliminate the weapons on which strategic deterrence has rested and those who see the Soviet nuclear buildup as a challenge that must be met with increased armaments. They reflect, as well, on the conceptual tension between eliminating nuclear weapons and answering the question of how defense can be managed in the nuclear era. Their contributions are at times compelling, at times frustrating, but at all times informative and of critical importance.

Roman Kolkowicz is professor of political science at the University of California, Los Angeles. **Neil Joeck** is a research fellow at the Center for International and Strategic Affairs, University of California, Los Angeles.

This book is also in the
Studies in International and Strategic Affairs Series
of the Center for International and Strategic Affairs,
University of California, Los Angeles

A list of the other titles in this series can be found at the back of the book.

JX
1974
.A768855
1984

Arms Control and International Security

edited by Roman Kolkowicz and Neil Joeck

Westview Press / Boulder and London

GOSHEN COLLEGE LIBRARY
GOSHEN, INDIANA

Westview Special Studies in International Relations

All rights reserved. No part of this publication may be reproduced or transmitted in any form or by any means, electronic or mechanical, including photocopy, recording, or any information storage and retrieval system, without permission in writing from the publisher.

Copyright © 1984 by The Regents of the University of California

Published in 1984 in the United States of America by Westview Press, Inc., 5500 Central Avenue, Boulder, Colorado 80301; Frederick A. Praeger, President and Publisher

Library of Congress Cataloging in Publication Data
Main entry under title:
Arms control and international security.
  (Westview special studies in international relations)
(Studies in international and strategic affairs series)
  Bibliography: p
  Includes index.
  1. Arms control—Addresses, essays, lectures.
2. Atomic weapons and disarmament—Addresses, essays,
lectures. 3. Security, International—Addresses,
essays, lectures. 4. Nuclear nonproliferation—Addresses,
essays, lectures. I. Kolkowicz, Roman. II. Joeck,
Neil. III. Series. IV. Series: Studies in interna-
tional and strategic affairs series.
JX1974.A768855   1984   327.1'74   83-16801
ISBN 0-86531-662-7
ISBN 0-86531-663-5 (pbk.)

Printed and bound in the United States of America

5   4   3   2   1

Contents

Part 3
Arms Control and Technology

Part 4
Arms Control and International Security:
Europe and the Soviet Union

Part 5
The Alternative to Arms Control

Preface

If this planet is ever ravaged by a nuclear war—if the survivors of that devastation can endure the fire, poison, chaos, and catastrophe—I do not want one of those survivors to ask another, "How did it all happen?" and to receive the incredible reply: "Ah, if only one knew."

—John F. Kennedy

The problem of arms control is akin to the task of a modern Sisyphus. No sooner do diplomats climb down the superpower mountain with treaties in hand than they must turn around and begin the climb again in a whole new negotiating process. And while the diplomats are talking, governments are building newer and more powerful weapons that further threaten international peace and stability and exacerbate the diplomatic efforts to achieve viable arms control. McGeorge Bundy portrayed this as a "curious and distressing paradox,"[1] and nuclear physicist Bernard Feld revealed a scientist's pessimism in describing the arduous process of "conceiving" an arms control agreement as one whose "offspring, when not aborted, is more likely to resemble a mouse."[2]

This paradox of arms control was most evident in the past decade—a decade characterized by peaceful and stable relations between the United States and the Soviet Union, by intensive diplomatic efforts to reach an end to the arms race and to enhance stability in various parts of the globe; and yet equally characterized by intensive arms development, arms production, and arms deployment as well as escalating arms sales in the most incendiary regions of the world. The weapons developed and deployed in this past decade are more deadly, more precise, and more costly than ever before and are indicative of the escalating momentum of the arms race.

What is becoming increasingly apparent to most thinking men and women is the essential futility of ever-escalating arms programs that provide no commensurate gains in national security or international stability. This sense of futility was expressed by Robert McNamara when he asserted that "unlike any other era in military history, today a substantial superiority of weapons does not effectively translate into political control or diplomatic leverage."[3] McGeorge Bundy echoed this judgment in saying that "the same leaders who know these terrible weapons must never be used, and who do not run the foolish risks of nuclear gamesmanship abroad, still do not hesitate to authorize system after system."[4]

The motives for engaging in arms control are complex and ambiguous and involve a multitude of technological, military, political, economic, and psychological factors that are frequently at odds with one another. Indeed, the impetus for arms control is fragile and ephemeral—circumstances favoring the initiation of such negotiations today may be rapidly overtaken by events tomorrow, by the inexorable march of technology and shifts in the political milieu. The fundamental tension between arms control and arms racing reflects a tension between the demands of national security and the aspirations of international stability. In the international system marked by threat and distrust, national leaders tend to seek security and influence in their own military power. This sense of insecurity, of external threat, and thus of the need to remain militarily strong is clearly expressed in Soviet thought: Lenin taught his disciples that "everything is a phantom except power"; Stalin maintained that the "essential question" is, "Who will defeat whom?"; and Khrushchev expressed his doubts about arms control in saying: "Some people watch us with greedy eyes and think how they can disarm us. But what would happen if we disarmed? We would certainly be torn to pieces."[5] And yet, despite its evident mistrust and "kto-kovo" mentality, the Soviet Union continues to express strong interest in arms control negotiations.

The earlier euphoric expectations of U.S.-Soviet arms control negotiations (and of détente) have given way to more sober and more realistic assessments—a sense of pessimism is replacing the pervasive optimism of only a decade ago. A national and international debate is emerging, propelled by a growing popular literature on nuclear war, on how to prevent it, and, if that fails, on how to deal with it. The Unthinkable has become, if not less frightening, then urgently more important to understand. It was in the spirit of this need to understand that the University of California sponsored the Conference on International Security and Arms Control. The conference was only part of a comprehensive effort initiated by the president of the university, David Saxon, who asked a committee,[6] under the chairmanship of Professor Herbert York, to assist him in the development of a university-wide program for the study of problems of international security and arms control. After extensive deliberations and consultations with faculty, students, the Board of Regents, and former Governor Edmund G. Brown, Jr., and his staff, the York Committee submitted its recommendation for the establishment of a University Institute on Global Conflict and Cooperation.

The Conference on International Security and Arms Control was proposed by the York Committee to inaugurate the university's effort toward an understanding of international security and arms control, and the Center for International and Strategic Affairs at UCLA was selected as the host institution. Distinguished scholars, experts, and public figures from all over the United States and abroad participated in the conference, which was open to the public. This provided an opportunity for the audience to question and debate the participants and resulted in frequently spirited exchanges not only between the audience and the panelists, but among the participants themselves. In six sessions, the conference participants addressed questions of the current status of arms control and international security, the impact of technology on arms control, proposals for the future of arms control measures and negotiations, the regional dimensions of arms control, and security in Europe and the Middle East,[7] finally concluding with a public lecture on the historical failings of disarmament and arms control and a proposal for alternative approaches. The editors of this volume agreed not to attempt any analytical assessments or summaries of the presentations, but to let them stand on their own to represent the wide diversity of subjects relevant to arms control.

In reading through the papers and comments presented at the conference, one is struck again by the skepticism concerning the prospects for arms control. This sense of lowered expectations motivated me to testify recently before a U.S. Senate committee concerned with the future of arms control and to recall my earlier rather pessimistic projections of the likely achievements of SALT, which I had made to a similar Senate committee a decade ago.[8] This led to a rather melancholy exchange during which Senator Cranston commented: "It isn't often that predictions stand up as well as those you have made . . . before the Senate Foreign Relations Committee ten years ago. I wish you had been wrong"; and I responded: "So do I. . . . The future of arms control will depend on new approaches, and upon mutual recognition of the futility of past policies and assumptions. For as Santayana warned us, those who do not remember the past are doomed to repeat it."[9]

In the final analysis, one wants to agree with the sentiments expressed by David Saxon when he said that ending the arms race and securing international stability were not "simple problems with simple answers, but rather formidable in their difficulty."[10] He remained nevertheless convinced that Andrei Sakharov was right in saying: "There is a need to create ideals even when you can't see any route by which to achieve them, because if there are no ideals, then there can be no hope, and then one would be completely in the dark."[11]

Roman Kolkowicz

Notes

1. McGeorge Bundy, "To Cap the Volcano," *Foreign Affairs*, vol. 48, no. 1, 1969, p. 14.
2. Bernard Feld, *A Voice Crying in the Wilderness: Essays on the Problems of Science and World Affairs* (Oxford: Pergamon Press, 1979), p. 162.
3. Robert S. McNamara, *Washington Post*, September 19, 1967.
4. Bundy, "To Cap the Volcano."
5. U.S. Senate, Subcommittee on Arms Control, International Law and Organization of the Committee on Foreign Relations, "ABM, MIRV, SALT, and the Nuclear Arms Race" (Washington, D.C.: U.S. Government Printing Office, 1970).
6. In addition to York, University of California, San Diego, the committee included the following members: Roger Batzel, Lawrence Livermore National Laboratory; Donald Kerr, Los Alamos National Laboratory; Roman Kolkowicz, University of California, Los Angeles; John Lewis, Stanford University; Michael May, Lawrence Livermore National Laboratory; and Carl Rosberg, University of California, Berkeley.
7. The presentations from the panel on the Middle East are not included in this volume.
8. U.S. Senate, Committee on Foreign Relations, "Strategic Arms Limitation Agreements," June/July 1972.
9. U.S. Senate, Subcommittee on Arms Control, Oceans, International Operations and Environment of the Committee on Foreign Relations, January 1982, p. 118.
10. David Saxon, "On the Pursuit of International Security," in *Arms Control in Transition: Proceedings of the Livermore Arms Control Conference*, W. Heckrotte and G. C. Smith, eds. (Boulder, Colo.: Westview Press, 1983), p. 177.
11. *Sakharov Speaks*, Harrison E. Salisbury, ed. (New York: Alfred A. Knopf, 1974), p. 73.

Acknowledgments

As director of the host institution at the time of the conference, I would like to take this opportunity to express my appreciation for the strong support given to the conference by President Saxon, Professor York, and the other members of the York Committee; and to the Ford Foundation, which provided partial funding for the conference. At UCLA, the staff of the Center, particularly Gerri Page and Leslie Rollins, responded admirably to the challenge of organizing a major international conference. Becky Goodman also provided timely editorial assistance. And last, but certainly not least, special recognition for his outstanding efforts is due my coeditor, Neil Joeck, whose contribution to the organizational aspects of the conference and to the editing of this volume was invaluable.

R. K.

Part 1

The Current Situation in Arms Control and International Security

1
Security Without Order: Nuclear Deterrence and Crisis Management in the 1980s

Christoph Bertram

A remarkable military—as opposed to a political—stability between East and West characterizes international security today. This balance shows its familiar robustness in the nuclear strategic field. The conventional balance in the defined areas of East-West deterrence in Europe and the Far East favors the Soviet Union on most indicators, but the risk of any conflict becoming nuclear continues to be a major deterrent.

Two ambiguities stand out in this picture. For one, the Soviet advantage in theater nuclear forces, while impressive, cannot easily be translated into a military advantage given the absence of any real likelihood that nuclear conflict could remain limited. Soviet theater nuclear improvements are, however, undermining the credibility of NATO's nuclear forces for deterrence and providing justification for NATO's Long-Range Theater Nuclear Force Modernization Program.

The second ambiguity concerns extra-European military contingencies, in particular the Gulf region. (Central America—for all the international emotions it generates—is not an issue of international security unless the United States decides to make it one.) The Soviet geographic advantage in the Gulf region is such that the West cannot establish military equality but instead must rely on the Soviet Union's recognition that central Western security interests are at stake there and on the credibility of overall deterrence. Although this requires some Western military intervention capability, it does not require the capability to fight and win a regional conflict with the Soviets.

Effective Deterrence

This rather relaxed view of the military balance depends, of course, on a belief in the continuing relevance of nuclear deterrence. Deterrence has worked in the past, but it is not easy to attribute the absence of war to one cause alone. Indeed, there are many reasons why war has not broken out between East and West since the nuclear age began. Perhaps the Soviet Union has had no serious interest in attacking. Perhaps it has not been in a position to attack with any confidence; after all, widespread Western notions of conventional Soviet superiority have often been influenced by the tendency to compare the other side's strengths with one's own weaknesses, rather than to compare strengths with strengths and weaknesses with weaknesses. And perhaps the Soviet Union felt *itself* threatened and was just building up what it regarded as an adequate defense.

There may be more reasons, but none is fully convincing in itself or in combination with others *unless* the threat of nuclear war is brought in. After all, Europe did not have a long tradition of peacefulness before the first nuclear device was detonated. On the contrary, the thirty-seven-year period of warlessness which today separates us from that detonation is an exception, not a rule, in Europe's troubled history. Moreover, these thirty-seven years have not been without conflict potential: a divided Germany, an exposed city of Berlin, the overthrow of governments in Eastern Europe, Soviet intervention in neighboring countries, ideological and political confrontation between East and West, rapidly changing military technology, the permanent presence of massive armed forces on both sides, the language of deterrence.

And yet, war has not broken out—probably because war in the nuclear age and between nuclear powers clearly has no winners, only losers. If nuclear deterrence has achieved this, it has been an effective instrument for keeping the peace. As the only empirical data we have on nuclear deterrence, this cannot be taken lightly. Many people claim that our security would be enhanced if only nuclear weapons could be disinvented or banned, but the experience of the past thirty-seven years suggests that the existence of nuclear weapons has prevented, not promoted war.

Will this continue to be the case? Nobody can be sure, of course, but the popular view that nuclear war is becoming more likely is not based on particularly convincing propositions. One proposition is that the passage of time alone makes nuclear war more likely because as we become more accustomed to the nuclear age we may forget how terrible nuclear weapons are. The persistence of antinuclear movements, however, particularly among the young, negates this proposition. As for the possibility of a nuclear accident, electronic devices have reduced that danger, and all states possessing nuclear weapons have taken great pains to ensure that political leadership alone will decide whether or not the nuclear threshold is passed. The accidents today are computer failures, and one cannot dismiss them lightly, particularly if they should occur at the height of an international crisis. But all computer failures that I am aware of have not overcome human incredulity that a nuclear attack could occur out of the blue; the failures have not, therefore, led anywhere close to the irreversible step of launching a nuclear strike—the nuclear caution prevailed. And that caution is likely to be greater as the risk becomes greater. Parity between the two major powers, the ability by both sides to destroy the other *after* having been attacked by nuclear weapons, means an increase, not a decrease, in nuclear caution, and not even the greatest accuracy of delivery will change that. There is no way the nuclear attacker can assume that he will survive.

Limited War

But would that caution prevail if nuclear wars could be limited—if in other words, the major powers could use nuclear weapons without risking their own survival? Nobody knows the answer to that hypothetical question. But the likelihood of limiting a nuclear exchange to certain weapons or to certain territories is so remote that the question will remain hypothetical for the foreseeable future.

Nuclear war will be limited only if governments have the means to limit it. In fact, they do not have such means. Technically, limitation would depend on electronic installations (command and control) that would not survive a nuclear exchange and that are themselves likely targets for nuclear or nonnuclear preemption. Politically, limited war would depend on *both* sides agreeing to limit—at best a possibility for tacit conformity, but not a reliable basis for nuclear planning.

These technical and political obstacles mean one thing: Any side that launches a nuclear weapon against the other must assume that it now has lost control over the course of events. Thus escalation to the highest level of mutual nuclear destruction is inherent in the first use of any nuclear weapon. Another outcome would be a miracle, and miracles are not a basis for an assessment of the future.

To sum up this first thesis: (1) Nuclear deterrence *has* worked, and it will continue to work. (2) Deterrence *has not* become weaker; parity has made it stronger. (3) Since limited nuclear war is highly unlikely—if not impossible—deterrence will continue to apply also in the regional context as long as there is a reasonable possibility that nuclear weapons would be involved in any major conflict.

Unacceptable Ambiguities

Yet this is a thesis that seems to aim against many current convictions. Why should this be so? One reason is that people have difficulty discussing deterrence in terms that do not imply its failure. Rather than examining why deterrence has worked, analysts and critics look for reasons why it does *not* work, and they examine nuclear stability from the hypothetical perspective that nuclear war has actually broken out.

This tempting approach needs to be resisted. Nobody knows what will happen once deterrence fails. Would both sides, as the textbook strategists have it, resort immediately to devastating surprise attacks on the other? This is what the apostles of strategic bombing predicted before the outbreak of World War II. In fact, however, even *after* that war had been declared and hostilities started on a grand and irreversible scale, all parties to the war—including the aggressor Germany—showed marked reluctance to use strategic bombing for fear of reprisal!

The difference between peacetime calculations and wartime action is likely to be even more marked in the case of nuclear weapons, because they could lead not only to deadly reprisal but also to an immediate loss on control over events. Political leaders will, in all probability, bend over backward to avoid an early nuclear decision, and for a protracted phase the conflict will be a *drôle de guerre* indeed, with even conventional operations conducted in such a way that the other side need not feel pushed into the corner of nuclear retaliation.

This example underlines how totally unreliable it is to project measures taken to enhance deterrence in peacetime into the environment of nuclear war. The conceptual weakness of deterrence lies here: In order to be credible to the deterred, the deterror must make preparations to execute the conditional threat. But there is little analytical value in assuming that these measures will also be the guide for what will happen once deterrence fails. There is no automaticity of transmission; deterrence and its failure are fundamentally different situations.

The other reason why the argument for deterrence finds itself under critique lies, paradoxically, in the very robustness of nuclear deterrence. Deterrence is neither significantly strengthened by doubling or trebling the number of nuclear warheads, nor weakened by scrapping half of the superpowers' arsenals. Overkill does not make nuclear war more likely. Overkill capacities can be criticized as wasteful, which they often are, but not as a threat to peace, which they are not.

Although reassuring, this robustness of deterrence is also corrupting because it does not provide a sufficiently obvious limit of how much is enough. This combination of robustness and lack of clear limits made it possible, for instance, for the United States to adhere publicly, until the early 1970s, to a concept of minimum deterrence against cities when at the same time it was developing a nuclear arsenal more geared for selective nuclear strikes against military targets. It may also explain the simultaneity of Leonid Brezhnev's assurance in November 1981 that nuclear war cannot be limited, and the exposure that same month of an old Russian submarine carrying a nuclear device on a reconnaissance mission in Swedish waters.

These ambiguities of deterrence, which may be familiar to that small in-group of professional analysts, are in the long run unacceptable for two reasons: They frustrate arms control, and they undermine the political support necessary for democratic countries to continue relying on nuclear weapons for their security.

How Much Is Enough?

The ambiguities have produced concepts that are essentially open ended. The most obvious example is the concept of limited nuclear options. The conviction developed in the late 1960s that deterrence had to be refined to consider more limited nuclear use was not without some merits. Could a conventional war in Europe really be credibly deterred by an explicit U.S. threat of all-out nuclear war? Or was such a suicidal riposte void of deterrent credibility? These questions, however, were not accompanied by any criteria of sufficiency. Instead, helped along by the rapidly growing accuracy of nuclear delivery systems and by the proliferation of nuclear warheads, military planners proliferated limited-nuclear-option packages—on military installations, key economic concentrations, military and political command posts—always with the argument that it would be good to have additional options. The strategic analytical community provided the conceptual rationale for this attitude through the general conviction that nuclear weapons should be good for something more than just the last resort.

As a result, Western strategy (and probably Soviet strategy as well) has lost the important ability to answer the question, "How much is enough?" The inability to define what one needs for deterrence may not be a danger to deterrence, but it is a danger to arms control because one can only define what one does *not* need if one has first defined what one *does* need.

At the moment, Western strategic requirements are limited by the money that is available rather than by functional concepts. This tends to make arms control agreements both militarily arbitrary and politically vulnerable—arbitrary, and hence controversial, because there is no single logic to the agreements; politically vulnerable because to overcome military controversy governments have to oversell the political symbolism.

We have all witnessed this with SALT II, the treaty negotiated since 1973, finally signed in 1979, and then fallen victim in 1980 to the deterioration of U.S.-Soviet relations and the passions of the U.S. Senate.

Nuclear arms control has other problems, of course, and the instrument, which was hailed with so much genuine hope in the 1960s, has witnessed growing difficulties: of verification, of preventing circumvention, of catching up with the dynamics of technological change. But these are secondary difficulties. As long as the "How much is enough?" question remains open, we cannot make real progress toward effective, militarily defendable, and politically acceptable arms control.

Nuclear Weapons and Domestic Support

The other reason why the ambiguity of deterrence is unacceptable lies in the nature of democratic societies. It is difficult to ask people to live with the fact that their security is based on the ability to blow up the world and themselves with it. It is barely—and only barely—acceptable if it is clear that nuclear force will not be used to fight a war but only to deter war.

The currently dominant strategic school of thought has tended to blur this fundamental distinction. In its fascination with limited nuclear options, highly subtle scenarios of nuclear sparring, and counterforce missions, the strategy has not only provided legitimacy for the military's instinct to regard any weapon as an instrument in war, but has also created doubt about the determination to deter, and to deter only.

Significantly, these technocrats of nuclear theology have been more concerned with the effect of their concepts on the Soviet Union than on their own population. Nothing underlines this apolitical approach more than the very term designed to cover all potential uses of nuclear weapons short of a disarming first strike or a cataclysmic retaliation—warfighting. This term means anything from one to thousands of nuclear explosions. As a result, U.S. nuclear doctrine has perhaps scared the Soviets, but it has certainly scared our own population—not only in Europe but in the United States.

This is not the only, or even the determining, source of support for the peace movement in Europe. Other factors, from concern over President Reagan's bellicose rhetoric to fears about the economic future, have probably been at least as decisive in giving an impetus to the antinuclear movement in European countries. But the games that strategists have played in the past ten years have also caused many people to fear that nuclear war is becoming more likely and that the search for deterrence only leads us down the steep path to nuclear extinction.

The lesson for strategists in the West seems clear: One does not play around with deterrence with impunity. Even if a concept of elaborate and distinct nuclear options and limited nuclear exchanges were to enhance deterrence vis-à-vis the Soviet Union—and I have expressed my doubts on this earlier—it would not be a concept that governments in democratic countries could adopt. To do so would sooner or later invite such controversy in domestic political constituencies that nuclear decisions and policies would themselves lack credibility. A recent example is NATO's 1979 decision to modernize theater nuclear forces and negotiate weapons control at the same time. Because of the domestic controversy over nuclear weapons in many member countries, governments have great difficulty convincing the Soviet Union that NATO will in fact implement the 1979 decision unless the Soviets accept curbs on their own burgeoning nuclear forces. Perhaps the Reagan administration's claim that negotiations over strategic weapons will only succeed if we first build up U.S. strategic forces may invite a similar difficulty.

Criteria of Restraint

To promote arms control and to maintain the deterrent credibility of democratic governments, we need to reduce the ambiguities of deterrence. But how? I cannot pretend that I have the full answer, but let me sketch out what might be some sensible guidelines for sizing Western nuclear forces for the 1980s and 1990s. First, we need to recognize that, as McGeorge Bundy has recently put it, mutual assured destruction is a basic condition, not one doctrine among many, for the nuclear age. There is no getting away from the essential unusability of nuclear weapons for other than the most dire situations of national (or alliance) survival.

This does not mean, however, that the only option for nuclear planners should be massive retaliation. Because our political leaders must be able to respond at the level of attack and not be forced into suicidal responses, we need more than this one option—particularly in the Western Alliance if it wants to retain the deterrent effect of U.S. nuclear forces against a Soviet military attack in Europe.

Many people in Europe insist that the United States should do away with all U.S. nuclear weapons in Europe and instead threaten to use its strategic arsenal for the sake of Europe. This move would not increase Western deterrence; it would not be politically acceptable in the United States and hence not credible. If extending deterrence to its allies meant that the United States would immediately risk its own survival, no U.S. president could count on the necessary political support. Therefore, nuclear options that do not deliberately (even if perhaps inevitably) push the world into extinction are essential, although we do not need to engage in the proliferation of nuclear options and scenarios of the past decade. The robustness and primitiveness of deterrence mean that nuclear options below a cataclysmic response can also be rugged and rather primitive—and few in number.

A second reasonable guideline is that the requirement for nuclear forces should be dictated by the minimum performance needed for credible deterrence, not by the number of forces, or even the number of targets, the other side has. Both sides have forces significantly larger than needed for credible deterrence, and the trend toward more accurate nuclear delivery systems provides a capability for which there is no rational need. What, for instance, is the essential contribution of the thousands of cruise missiles that the United States wants to deploy in the mid-1980s? Or take two recent European examples: the British Trident 2 decision and the rationale behind NATO's nuclear modernization program. For the "last resort deterrent," which is all Britain can ever acquire, Trident 2 vastly exceeds requirements (as it does for the United States). Its deterrent effect will thus be continuously challenged by widespread political uneasiness, even if the Conservatives remain in power long enough to see the program through to completion.

The NATO modernization program for long-range theater nuclear force is equally controversial. Although a sensible program, by and large, many of its supporters have mistakenly justified it by arguing that this is the correct response to the Soviet SS-20 missile program. This is the old and useless tit-for-tat approach that merely calls for Western forces because of the existence of Eastern ones (and, no doubt, vice versa). The actual reason why the NATO program makes military sense is that a number of Soviet weapons introduced in recent years have tended to make the existing Western theater nuclear weapons vulnerable to nuclear or conventional preemption. This specific military requirement needs to be met, rather than a counter to the SS-20 missile.

But there is another lesson here about the need to stick to more rigid criteria of deterrence requirements. Such criteria have not been applied in NATO's *existing* theater nuclear posture. While some U.S. nuclear weapons in Europe obviously enhance the deterrent against a massive attack in Europe, it seems equally obvious that what we have in our arsenals is often of doubtful relevance to this task. Take NATO's heavy emphasis on battlefield nuclear weapons, for example. Over 50 percent of these weapons are linked to delivery means with ranges below thirty kilometers. Will the U.S. president with whom the nuclear release decision rests be prepared to pass the momentous threshold to nuclear war at a time when he still cannot judge whether an attack can be repulsed by conventional forces, and can he decide within the time pressures implied by such short distances? This also, incidentally, is the reason why the deterrence value of the neutron weapon is so questionable. Whatever its military effects in theory, it remains a battlefield nuclear weapon and hence subject to much the same limitations that make the present battlefield arsenal so doubtful for deterrence.

If *some* U.S. nuclear weapons contribute to an effective deterrent in Europe, then the question is not whether, but which, weapons are needed. Much of the present arsenal is largely unsuitable, highly vulnerable to attack or to being overrun, and dependent on totally unrealistic decision times. The most powerful argument in favor of the NATO modernization decision is that it will introduce less vulnerable weapons, with longer ranges, which means they can be stationed away from the battlefield. It will do that in numbers that are insufficient to constitute a serious strategic threat to the Soviet Union.

For the same reason, the "zero option" for theater nuclear forces, if obtained in the current Geneva negotiations, makes little military sense. Such an agreement would tend to lock the West into its old-fashioned and questionable posture of maintaining existing tactical nuclear weapons and would not permit a sensible modernization, together with a phasing out of old systems.

Finally, making deterrence respectable again means to be less ambiguous about what nuclear deterrence can actually achieve. Deterrence cannot prevent an invasion of Afghanistan. It cannot keep the Soviet Union, or any other country, from meddling in an Iranian civil war. It cannot make up for conventional military strength—in Europe or elsewhere. It *can* discourage planned, deliberate attacks where nuclear forces might become involved, but it cannot keep things from getting out of control and escalating from a minor to a major crisis. In other words, deterrence is a central, but not a sufficient, element of security in the nuclear age.

Crises Below Deterrence

Those who pretend that the prevention of an East-West war is the most urgent international task today are led by emotion rather than by analysis. They are also asking that the limited amount of political energy available be spent on a problem that does not yet require it, at the expense of others that do.

In fact, the danger of a major war is today no greater and, possibly, less than in the past. There is no likelihood of a major deliberate Soviet military attack against the West or—for the sake of symmetry—of a nuclear strike by the United States against the East. Furthermore, however important the specific imbalances in the overall force relationship, a military balance that discourages any direct military confrontation does exist today. In this most basic sense of balance, we have security.

What we do not have is the other ingredient of stability: international order. That lack is particularly visible in two areas of the world, Eastern Europe and the Middle East. In Eastern Europe—in Poland—the Soviet Union has again demonstrated its inability to develop a way to exert control while tolerating the political aspirations of the population. We must expect, therefore, more and not less unrest, and at more frequent intervals, in the Soviets' East European empire. Perhaps this unrest can be contained, repressed, localized, but perhaps it cannot. This could be the beginning of a slide into an unplanned, unwanted conflict in Europe that could spill across the East-West dividing line.

In the Middle East, the chances that the Camp David agreements offered are running out. For all governments in the region, the domestic political margin of maneuver becomes more circumscribed, as well as the ability to take bold initiatives of the kind President Anwar Sadat took in November 1977, which would be needed to break the deadlock. Israel's policy of creating strategic facts cannot succeed in producing a durable regional solution; instead, it is likely to breed the conditions for a future war. Such a war could scarcely be limited to the region and scarcely be controlled from the outside. Again there would be the real danger of drifting into international conflict.

Precisely because deterrence does *not* cover them, these two situations stand for a much more real danger to our security than a premeditated East-West war. In other words, we have the means to prevent the big, planned, unthinkable disaster; we do not have the means to meet the lesser, more likely crises that could suck us into war.

Here lies the major deficit of our security today. If a crisis of the kind suggested above should occur, the major powers would have to start from scratch. They do not have a functioning framework for effective dialogue today, and not even the Western Alliance—as demonstrated by the crises over Afghanistan, Iran, and now Poland—has been able to develop effective contingency planning. Instead, we have rhetorical posturing, threats and sanctions, a dialogue of the deaf across the East-West divide, and an alliance that, once a crisis erupts, seems more intent on showing its differences than manifesting its consensus.

We urgently need to develop effective East-West structures for the management of major international crises. Today they do not exist. The "hot line" between Moscow and Washington failed in the Afghanistan crisis. The European Security Conference has become too much of an open forum to hold much promise for discrete crisis communication. And the most obvious means—a direct summit meeting between the Soviet and the U.S. presidents—has been burdened with so much political symbolism that even agreeing to get together without preconditions will be seen as a concession by one and a gain for the other side.

Once a crisis is upon us, however, it is usually too late to set up the mechanism for crisis management. Then both the United States and the Soviet Union—particularly a new U.S. administration and a new and inexperienced leadership in Moscow—may be inclined to see such a crisis as a deliberate test by the other side in which firmness, not diplomatic subtlety, is required. That has the makings of crisis escalation, not crisis management.

What makes our present international condition so worrisome is this: We have the basic security of deterrence, but we have no order, and no instruments to promote order, in the crises that are sure to come. We are relying on little else than that rare commodity—the political instinct of common sense. That is not a comforting prospect. Setting up procedures for effective East-West crisis management is therefore the most pressing task of international security today.

Creating these procedures will require deterrence and dialogue, respect for the power of the other and confidence in one's own power, and a sense that the task can be met. For all this, the reassurance of deterrence is essential; no major power will embark on the road to compromise if it fears for its basic security. The utopian wish to see nuclear weapons disappear and the doomsday emotions of supposedly imminent end games are recipes for avoiding the feasible, for overlooking the possible, and for neglecting the necessary.

Challenges to Deterrence

Deterrence today is clearly robust and effective, but we need clearer criteria for what is militarily required both to regain the respectability of deterrence in democratic societies and to promote an effective search for arms control.

Will deterrence remain robust and effective in the indefinite future? Nobody knows. The robustness of deterrence depends, after all, on the credibility of the means and on the willingness to invoke them. These are not static conditions. What are some possible changes beyond the 1980s?

The first category of changes depends on technology. Deterrence is robust today essentially because nothing of what technology has generated in the last thirty years has fundamentally altered the basic fact that nuclear wars cannot be won, only lost, and because any direct military conflict between East and West contains the risk of becoming nuclear. That may change. There might be, one day, technically reliable ways of controlling nuclear war, thus blurring the distinction between nuclear and nonnuclear weapons. Alternatively, and perhaps more probable, the separation between usable conventional and unusable nuclear weapons might become more pronounced as improved nonnuclear technologies take over part of the spectrum of destruction hitherto reserved for nuclear weapons. The barrier to all kinds of military conflict that nuclear deterrence has so far provided could become eroded in either case.

The second, more political, category of changes affects the Western Alliance and the notion of extended deterrence. This Western Alliance is, in the history of alliance, a real anomaly. It is not only based on the assumption that the security of allies is important enough for the other members to go to war in their support—that is a familiar component of traditional alliances—but on the assumption that the security of the European allies is important enough for the United States to risk its own nuclear extinction. Small wonder that the arch-traditionalist Charles de Gaulle found it impossible to understand! This extraordinary Atlantic bargain can be maintained only if the alliance is more than merely a military pact, if it is built not only on the negative—the fear of a common enemy—but on the positive, that is, the trust and confidence of being in the same boat culturally, economically, and historically.

On both sides of the Atlantic, we are witnessing an erosion of this trust and confidence, and thus of the deterrence identity on which the alliance depends. For many people in Europe, the future seems to lie in a greater distance from the two superpowers; for many in the United States, it lies in a greater independence of action, not in "entangling alliances." If this trend continues, the Western Alliance may survive as a conventional military arrangement, but it will not survive as the collectivity of risk on which the U.S. nuclear commitment can be based. The consequence is unlikely to be greater stability in Europe.

Deterrence is not immutable; what works in the 1980s may not work beyond the 1980s. However, we do have the basic security of deterrence today, and we can assess, without panic and with the patience of reason, how to maintain and adjust it. That is far from ideal. But it is a much better chance than what was available to earlier generations in this century.

2
Some Thoughts About
Unilateral Moderation

McGeorge Bundy

For reasons that lie deep in the state of mind of the present administration in Washington, arms control negotiations with the Soviet Union, whether on intermediate nuclear forces or on strategic arms reductions, are almost sure to go nowhere. The U.S. opening positions in both negotiations are designed for their immediate political value, both in Europe and in the United States. They also reflect deep-seated and honest concerns of government leaders on both sides of the Atlantic—in the European case about Soviet SS-20s, and in the U.S. case about Soviet SS-18s. Negotiating these two forces down or out is something that governments would very much like to achieve.

In that sense, one cannot question the sincerity of the beliefs behind these opening positions. What *can* be questioned, however, is whether the proposals are negotiable or seriously intended to be negotiable. The arguments thus far put forward by the proponents of the U.S. position do not include any persuasive explanation of the reasons that would induce the Soviet government to accept the dismantling of modern weapons systems—obviously highly valued by its own military leadership—in return for the much more modest and less central limitations that U.S. proposals would require on the Western side. Without dramatic changes in the U.S. position, therefore, the prospect for a satisfactory negotiation is thin.

Such dramatic changes are exactly what it is unreasonable to expect from the present administration. All the evidence suggests that the opening positions for both Intermediate Nuclear Forces (INF) talks and the Strategic Arms Reduction Talks (START) were put together with difficulty in a process of interdepartmental bargaining and final resolution by the president, a process only too familiar from earlier administrations. What also seems clear is that while the president has been able to function as a referee at the necessary moments of decision, he has not functioned as a catalytic leader. In almost two years, he has not shown any serious concern at any time for the negotiability of his proposals. Such leadership as the president has exercised has been for the purpose of ensuring opening positions that meet immediate political requirements. There is no sign whatever of any intent to take operational leadership in the process of negotiation.

The apparent absence of such intent is a matter of great importance in assessing the prospects for new agreements. The long, mixed record of efforts to get international agreements on nuclear weapons demonstrates plainly that one essential element in any successful negotiation is the direct and intense engagement of the president of the United States himself. Such engagement is not sufficient to produce agreement, but it is clearly necessary. We would not have the Limited Test Ban Treaty without the direct personal efforts of John F. Kennedy; we would not have the Nonproliferation Treaty of 1968 without the personal decision of Lyndon Johnson that its achievement should be a matter of high priority; we would not have the Antiballistic Missile Treaty and the SALT I Agreement without Richard Nixon. The unratified treaties of later years are also the result of direct presidential decisions. Conversely, where presidents have been unwilling to take a firm lead, agreements have been elusive. In different ways, and in spite of personal good intentions, both Harry Truman and Dwight Eisenhower failed on this front.

It is always possible that any president will change his priorities, and we know from the remarkable political energy displayed by President Reagan on domestic economic policy in 1981 that he is capable of effective leadership when he has clear-cut goals in which he deeply believes. But the changes, both of attitude and of style, that would be required to make him an active leader in the pursuit of a negotiated arms agreement seem larger than any changes made before in the behavior of any occupant of the White House.

A further obstacle to change lies in the fact that the executive branch is heavily populated, at high levels of the departments and agencies primarily concerned, by hard-line ideologues with a clear record of hostility to past agreements and deep-seated suspicion of any compromise with Moscow. The most striking examples of such men happen to be in the Arms Control and Disarmament Agency (ACDA) itself. Very few disinterested observers would pick Eugene Rostow, Paul Nitze, and Edward Rowny as the men most likely to work their way unaided toward a sound compromise with Moscow. This is not at all because they are insincere in seeking such agreement or because they lack technical competence. Paul Nitze may be the most experienced of all U.S. students of these questions, and he is certainly one of the most sincere. But it is an understatement to say that he proceeds from a worst-case analysis of Soviet intentions and capabilities—not a promising starting point for the management of a negotiation.

Furthermore, Mr. Nitze is by no means the most rigid member of the administration. There are still more passionate ideologues among civilians in high places at the Pentagon, and the secretary of defense himself, Caspar Weinberger, has shown a simplistic rigidity on such matters, which contrasts notably with the state of mind of such critically important predecessors as Harold Brown and Robert McNamara. It is too soon to estimate whether any substantive change in the balance of the counsel reaching the president will emerge from the appointment of George Shultz as secretary of state, but it is not too soon to note the striking fact that as the administration worked out its opening position for START, the principal advocates of moderation were the joint chiefs of staff.

This unpromising situation in the U.S. executive branch has parallels in Moscow; it is not a wholly asymmetrical difficulty. Some attitudes in Moscow always tend to make agreement difficult—attitudes about secrecy and inspection, attitudes about the discussion of planned deployments, attitudes toward the process of negotiation itself, and attitudes toward truth. The Soviet government is very often part of the problem, and yet necessarily it must also be part of any solution. The actions of that government in Afghanistan and in Poland have not contributed toward a favorable prospect for reliable agreement in any field, and we must add now that the beginning of a period of transition away from the age of Brezhnev to that of Yuri Andropov adds uncertainty and probably some measure of immobility to the Soviet position. For the Soviet government, as for our own, there is a certain political safety in the adoption of negotiating positions that seem politically defensible in the short run and that do not call for hard decisions to put new limits on one's own forces.

All in all, when one considers the situation as it actually is in Washington and in Moscow, the prospect of any large-scale new international agreement in the next two years appears extraordinarily small. Nor will this prospect be significantly changed by the rising strength of popular movements against nuclear weapons in Western Europe and now in the United States as well. Those movements can and will be effectively contained in the short run by the cosmetic positions available to skillful governments. Cosmetic skills of this sort abound both in Moscow and in Washington.

We can therefore expect that both sides will deploy considerable skills in efforts to show their own positions to be reasonable, and in the short run, at least, each side will be sufficiently successful to avoid unacceptable political damage where it matters most—in U.S. public opinion as a whole to the U.S. government, and in the internal political balance of authority in Moscow to the Soviet government. The negotiations in Geneva promise to be nothing more than a propaganda battle during the present U.S. administration. Although we can wish otherwise, we cannot ignore the realities, which presently seem very large and strong.

But even though early new agreements are not in sight, there is also no prospect that the limited achievements of SALT I and SALT II will be heavily eroded in the next few years. Both the ABM Treaty and the broad provisions of the SALT II Agreement will probably remain in force. Given the earlier positions of the president himself and the men around him, this conclusion is interesting. The treaty that Ronald Reagan once found fatally flawed is now a treaty that he proposes to observe as long as the Soviet Union observes it too. There is room for amusement at the intellectual contortions required to sustain both of these positions, but there is also room for satisfaction in the result.

Moreover, it is a comforting fact that there seems to be no serious political disagreement with the present position of the administration. The U.S. Senate, in accepting this position, is in the process of setting an interesting and constructive precedent. What the Senate is doing is to assert by its own inaction that it is willing to tolerate the observance of an unratified agreement for an indefinite period as long as it sees no reason to challenge the administration on principle or to press for some specific action that would violate the agreement. This precedent may well have considerable importance in the future. It reinforces the earlier precedent under which the SALT I agreement was extended by unchallenged executive action, and it widens the prospect that arms control agreements may be achievable by less rigorous processes than those of treaty ratification.

Thus no significant change, either up or down, can be expected in the existing pattern of international agreements on arms control, and precisely because of this, now is a good time for thinking again, and thinking hard, about what nuclear weapons are good for. When the time comes—as it surely will—that the two governments are really ready for serious negotiations, we may well need new ideas of what to negotiate about.

A further reason for reassessing the U.S. position is that recent debate among us has tended to distract us from the underlying realities of the world of modern nuclear weapons. As Christoph Bertram pointed out in the previous chapter, debate among experts has tended to be governed excessively by a concern with the prospects and problems of limited nuclear war. Desmond Ball, who has written the most powerful single paper on the difficulties of controlling nuclear war, concludes that it is foolish to have any great confidence in our ability to exercise such control. Bertram also maintains that when we allow ourselves to become heavily occupied with the ways and means of having second, third, and fourth rounds of nuclear escalation, we are missing the point that the fundamental object of these weapons is to deter, and we may not adequately consider just what it is we think they should deter.

There is a certain cyclical tendency in this country to give in to the temptation to say that nuclear weapons are not all that different from other weapons of war. One of the most sensible of U.S. presidents, Dwight Eisenhower, once said that, but he said very different things earlier and later. It is clearly a mistake to make plans that call for the early use of nuclear weapons on any battlefield, and for that reason the administration's evident affection for the neutron bomb raises grave questions. It is a self-inflicted political wound of no small importance to give others the impression that we contemplate such early use. There are other ways of thinking about the matter, and perhaps those other ways can give us better guidance on the question of how much is enough on the U.S. side—better guidance than we get from current discussions of limited nuclear war, or from our own tendency to think that if the other side has a given weapon, we had better get it too.

This tendency is reinforced by one of the unfortunate legacies of the SALT I debate. As a consequence of that debate, the U.S. government became committed to something very vague, described as "essential equivalence," which is often read in the Congress, and perhaps in the country, as meaning that if the Soviet Union has very large weapons, which it does, then we are in some sense inferior and should be doing something (the MX missile is the principal something at the moment) to get back to "equivalence."

Another way to look at it is this: For many years, and certainly since the late 1960s, the United States has had a strategic nuclear stockpile that is much larger and much more destructive than necessary and entirely adequate in its survivability. The kinds of things for which nuclear weapons can be used, in an age in which the Soviet Union has the kind of forces it now has, are few. Thirty years ago, when Robert Oppenheimer first had the idea, it made some sense to have tactical weapons in Europe and to plan quite explicitly for their early use. It no longer makes sense to do that. A policy of no *early* use, and over time no *first* use, of nuclear weapons would be much better. The basic reason for this conviction has been well stated by a distinguished U.S. military officer, General A. S. Collins, who said that it is very hard indeed to think of any use of nuclear weapons by one side that does not produce a nuclear reply by the other side. In General Collins's words, "There are no one-sided wars between superpowers."

If that is true, then it is going to be even more likely in the future than in the past that any president called upon to give approval for use of nuclear weapons will think very hard indeed before he gives that approval. That is the lesson of history on the subject, and the present situation only reinforces the prospect of great presidential caution.

As far as we know, with the possible exception of messages sent to Peking by the Eisenhower administration in the last stages of the struggle for a truce in the Korean War, there has been no direct threat by the United States to initiate the use of nuclear weapons since Nagasaki. There have certainly been situations, like the Berlin crisis of 1958–1962, in which our adversaries have had to consider the possibility that we would use such weapons, but, again with the possible exception of Korea in 1953, no president has made a direct threat of such action.

Caution on this front will be stronger—not weaker—in the future, and on this point (as distinct from the question of attitudes toward arms control negotiations) the attitude of a president is not likely to be governed primarily by the ideas and notions by which he was attracted as a critic or a candidate. People who sit in that White House office tend to reach the conclusion that President Kennedy reached–that any U.S. decision to make a first use of nuclear weapons would be a most enormous confession of political failure. Today it would carry with it risks of uncontrollable escalation that are as visible as they are incalculable. Thus it makes sense to frame our nuclear policy in terms of a central intent to use these weapons only to deter their use by others. Although there is a quite special case on the central front in Europe, a policy of no-first-use is the right one there too, and any necessary balancing conventional strength is attainable at an entirely acceptable cost. The logical conclusion, then, is that we should move toward a doctrine of no-first-use, in the belief that workable alternatives are available.

Next, we should examine more carefully than we have yet done just what kind of *second* use would ever be desirable. And here—since we must accept the argument of Desmond Ball and others that we really cannot tell what any kind of nuclear war would be like—we shall find ourselves forced to the position that any second-use posture must limit itself to relatively simple, relatively robust choices. In addition, in framing such choices we do not need to be able to match exactly what may have been done in someone else's first use. Indeed, a second-strike deterrent policy might well be based on a quite different proposition: namely, that the continuing capacity for a *lesser* reply would be amply adequate for a confident posture of deterrence.

Such a proposition makes sense for several reasons. For one, it is a characteristic of these weapons that for rational men an exchange in which one's own side receives only one-fifth of the damage that one has done to others would still be a most unfavorable affair. These are not either zero-sum or positive-sum weapons; they are negative-sum weapons, and a relatively small reply, indeed even a small chance of a small reply (using the word "small" in the context of the enormity of these weapons systems as they stand) has great deterrent force. Mutual assured destruction (MAD) is indeed a condition, not a theory. MAD is a fact, and it is nuclear-use theory that is mostly NUTS.

A quite different acronym for an adequate deterrent capability would be ARREST—Adequate Repeatable Retaliation Ends Strike Temptation. The important word here is *repeatable*. We need to be able to prevent any government, even in its most adventurous moods, from supposing that it could win and end a strategic nuclear war by totally ending our own capacity for retaliation. That is a hard requirement, because it does mean endurable command and control, at least for relatively simple retaliatory purposes. Yet it is a much easier requirement than what is imposed by any supposition that we ourselves would wish to win such a war rather than simply end it. A posture of this kind could be sustained by much smaller forces, both in numbers and in megatonnage, than are now deployed. If properly defended and explained, this posture would be more acceptable to our own people. It is in a sense the smallest force that will provide adequate nuclear deterrence against nuclear attack in a world where these enormous systems do exist. At the same time, it would make clear an absence of intention to be the initiators—even by inadvertence, even in resistance to aggression—of a thermonuclear holocaust.

The proposal for a nuclear freeze is a subject of increasing public attention in our country now. As it stands, the proposal for a bilateral freeze is an important contribution to the debate, but it would be preferable to start with a doctrine of unilateral moderation, using criteria like the ones suggested here—or better ones. The difficulty with the freeze is that in its current political form it requires a bilateral and verifiable agreement. A verifiable freeze on testing, production, and deployment is a very large order and would require access to the Soviet Union at a level that is unprecedented. Moreover, many unanswered questions remain about the terms and conditions of a bilateral freeze; these could not be avoided in the actual process of negotiation. The freeze, as it stands, is a proposal for an agreement that might well turn out not to be negotiable; at best, it would be at least as complex as SALT itself has become. In addition, the very concept of such a freeze is obviously unacceptable to a majority of the present Senate and almost all of the present administration. There is, therefore, a further danger that unless advocates of the freeze think carefully and soberly about the way their proposal is presented as time goes on, it may help to divide Americans against one another rather than to produce an effective consensus for an attainable agreement.

Yet, at the same time, the basic objectives of the supporters of the freeze can be understood. They are not wrong in suggesting that the existing balance of thermonuclear forces is acceptable, and in time the argument they are making may possibly be translated into both unilateral decisions and negotiating proposals that can indeed command general national support. The freeze proposal as it stands has the simplicity—even the crudeness—required for easy public understanding. There is no reason to suppose that it cannot evolve into a policy that has the combination of unilateral boldness and bilateral subtlety that will be necessary for real progress.

Finally, in spite of the intensity of our current debates, there is a general agreement that we are not in fact in a period in which the danger of intercontinental thermonuclear war is unusually high. In fact, a certain rough-hewn strength is evident in the state of mutual nuclear deterrence that exists between the Soviet Union and the United States. While stockpiles on both sides are obviously excessive, it remains true that the existence of survivable weapons in large numbers does give a certain stability to our situation, as Thomas Schelling pointed out some twenty years ago.

Although there is no occasion for any complacency, neither is it right to approach the question as one that has some unprecedented aura of crisis about it in the mid-1980s.

Discussion of Part 1

Desmond Ball

According to McGeorge Bundy, the record of the last thirty years demonstrates that no U.S. president would find it easy to initiate the use of nuclear weapons, that nuclear weapons are not ordinary instruments of war, and that they are therefore not very usable. Christoph Bertram believes that nuclear weapons are usable only in the sense of deterring direct attacks on the U.S. homeland and when the Western Alliance is itself threatened. But it seems that the facts of the last thirty to forty years argue otherwise.

Nuclear weapons have in fact been used. They were first used thirty-nine years ago in Hiroshima and Nagasaki, and they have been used, in a much more instrumental and conditional sense, as the very basis of postwar deterrence. They may not have been detonated in anger since 1945, but the threat of such use has been an essential component of deterrence. This is a utility that no U.S. president has considered disavowing. Indeed, on at least two dozen occasions since 1945, the highest U.S. national security officials have considered using nuclear weapons is some more positive fashion. The instances include Berlin, Korea, the offshore-islands crisis, Laos, Cuba, Dien Bien Phu, Khe Sanh, and so on. In all of these cases, the U.S. president decided against using nuclear weapons. Although in most of these cases, the proposals came from only a very few of the many U.S. officials involved, the fact remains that consideration was given to their use.

Furthermore, despite the disclaimings of U.S. declaratory policy, the history of nuclear development over the past three decades has been one of consistent attempts to make nuclear weapons usable. These attempts include the development of tactical nuclear weapons in the 1950s, the development of smaller strategic nuclear weapons and more precise means of delivery in the 1960s and 1970s, the development of strategic concepts and doctrines for limited and controlled nuclear warfighting, and the development of regional nuclear options. The 40,000 potential targets in the current Single Integrated Operational Plan (SIOP) are one extreme manifestation of this development. As long as these trends continue, efforts at arms control will inevitably prove futile. Such trends have destroyed the very criteria upon which arms control can be based.

There used to be something of a consensus to the effect that while nuclear weapons should not be usable for nuclear warfighting, they do have a proper and legitimate utility in providing deterrence. That was a different concept of deterrence, which was seen then as the ability to threaten unacceptable damage under all circumstances. Robert McNamara defined it in the 1960s as the ability to suffer a Soviet first strike and then retaliate so as to kill a quarter to a third of the Soviet population and destroy from two-thirds to three-quarters of Soviet industry. Such a formulation made it relatively easy to determine the question, "How much is enough?" Thus, under the most conservative assumptions, the United States required an ability to deliver about 400 equivalent megatons against the Soviet target base.

But now the very concept of deterrence has changed. Instead of being counterposed to defense or to strategic warfighting, which were considered inimical to deterrence in the 1960s, current statements from the administration, as well as the analytic community, point out that defense and warfighting capabilities are now essential ingredients of deterrence. Without them, it is argued, deterrence is not credible. In this formulation, there is no conceptual way to determine how much is enough; there is always a requirement for more, and for more yet again.

The only way to get off this treadmill is to ask whether in fact nuclear weapons *are* usable in the warfighting scenarios that form the basis of current defense planning. Insofar as they do have some utility, might there not be other ways of satisfying the same utility within reasonable resource limits and at less risk should deterrence fail?

The fact of the matter is that despite developments in technology and policy over the last few decades, strategic nuclear weapons are no more usable now than they were before. The situation, however, has become much more dangerous because now many so-called strategists, and so-called realists, believe that they have in fact become more usable. The notion of limited or controlled nuclear war is central to this argument, although the possibility of controlling a nuclear war exists only in the eyes of the deluded.

There are several reasons why limited nuclear war is impossible. First is the vulnerability of the command, control, communications, and real-time intelligence systems (C^3I) that would be necessary for controlling a nuclear exchange. These systems are more vulnerable than the forces they were designed to support. Attempting to insulate strategic C^3, as the current U.S. administration is doing, is not going to provide an answer because command and control systems by their very nature have some critical vulnerabilities that simply cannot be removed. The integrity of the systems needed to control a nuclear war would be the first casualty of any nuclear use.

Second, there is the question of collateral damage: Even very limited use of nuclear weapons involves massive casualties. Pure counterforce strategies could involve casualties as high as 20 million people, perhaps even 30 million, and in some estimates as many as 50 million. That is a strange definition of "limited" war, if those casualty estimates are indeed correct.

Third, the fog of battle would be the prevailing element in any nuclear exchange. Fourth is the question of Soviet doctrine; it takes two to keep a nuclear exchange controlled, and according to Soviet doctrine, the Soviets do not believe in playing these controlled, sequential escalatory games.

Granted, the United States needs to have capabilities for trying to contain a nuclear exchange once one has begun, no matter what the reason—accident, miscalculation, or whatever. Hence the development of a certain range of options should not be opposed. But it is dangerous as well as self-defeating to base policy on the ability to threaten, and then conduct, a limited nuclear war.

Why has the United States thought it necessary to adopt such a policy? The answer, of course, is extended deterrence. The threat of limited nuclear use is needed to deter Soviet action in Europe, in the first instance; but now that threat has been extended to Southwest Asia and to Northeast Asia. Extended deterrence based on such threatened use of nuclear weapons retains no credibility today. It must therefore be asked whether there are other ways of satisfying the objectives of extended deterrence. The most obvious possibility is through conventional forces, which entails enormous and numerous budgetary, political, and alliance problems associated with arriving at an adequate conventional deterrent posture. But if we are convinced that to threaten limited nuclear war is incredible, these problems must be viewed as a challenge to be overcome.

In the end, the control of nuclear weapons may only be possible by the development of more imaginative means of deploying and employing conventional forces. Only down this route will we find an answer to how much is enough at the nuclear level. This may not be a very attractive argument to many concerned citizens, but we must be realistic. Nuclear weapons can only be controlled by finding some other means of satisfying whatever utility they are perceived to possess. Before we can control the arms race, those means must be explored.

Hans Bethe

The dominant theme of Reagan administration rhetoric is that the Soviet Union is superior to the United States in nuclear weapons; therefore a buildup of our nuclear armaments must take priority over any negotiation of new arms control measures. Against this disturbing background, it is encouraging that Eugene Rostow, former director of the Arms Control and Disarmament Agency (ACDA), stated in an interview with the *New York Times* (March 21, 1982) that he is not aiming for nuclear weapons superiority, but merely for a credible second-strike force. Every paper in this collection supports this aim, and all past administrations of the United States believed in this concept and implemented it. But when we already have such a force, why do we need a buildup?

The mainstay of this second-strike capability is, of course, the ballistic missile submarine force. It is virtually impossible to detect and destroy all, or even a large fraction, of these submarines. At present, they carry a total of almost 600 missiles, with almost 5,000 warheads—more than half of all the warheads in the U.S. nuclear strategic force. In addition, we are installing cruise missiles on our B-52 bombers. Although land-based cruise missiles in Europe should by all means be avoided, it is a different matter with the bombers. Widely dispersed over many airfields, the bombers would take off on warning and provide a secure second-strike force in the most unlikely event of an all-out attack by Soviet ICBMs. Cruise missiles on these bombers can penetrate any presently known air defenses, and as the bombers do not have to penetrate the Soviet Union, they do not need all the electronic gadgets that the Air Force is fond of putting on them. It is even less necessary to have the B-1 bomber and still less to have the STEALTH bomber to follow that.

Then what is it that we do need? Accuracy? The cruise missiles are extremely accurate. And why is accuracy important in a second-strike force? Most military targets (like airfields, petroleum storage depots, depots of conventional armaments) are soft. The main hard target—the ICBM missile silo—will be empty if there is a first strike by the Soviets. In fact, large numbers of highly accurate nuclear weapons on our side would only encourage the Soviets to launch their ICBMs all at once in case of an all-out attack—a tactic surely not in our interest.

The fact is that we already have a credible, more than sufficient second-strike force; in this respect, our forces are superior to those of the Soviet Union. Although the Soviets have 950 submarine-launched missiles compared to our 580, they have only 1,900 warheads on those compared to our nearly 5,000. Numbers may not mean anything in this game, but the people who want to rearm in order to achieve equality with the Soviets maintain that numbers are important. And when we look at numbers, we are superior. The Soviets have nothing to balance our bomber-launched cruise missiles.

The Soviets have superiority only in land-based ICBMs, with 1,400 launchers compared to our 1,050, 5,500 warheads compared to our 2,100, and an even greater superiority in throwweight. But the "window of vulnerability" postulated by our Pentagon analysts means that our ICBM forces are vulnerable. If so, the Soviet forces are also vulnerable— even more so because a much larger fraction of their force is in ICBMs. Therefore, if there is a window of vulnerability, it's on the other side of the house. Soviet superiority in this area does not constitute a credible second-strike force.

The only purpose of nuclear weapons should be to ensure that the other side will not use nuclear weapons against you, and for this the only important requirement is a secure second-strike force. This we have, so we do not need a buildup of nuclear armaments, which can only make arms control more difficult in the future.

Command, control, and communications, however, should be improved. While we may not be able to rely on their survival, we must have them—at least in the beginning of a hypothetical nuclear war. Secure C^3 is not only in the interest of the country that has it but also in the interest of a potential enemy. It is an important requirement for avoiding accidental war.

Nuclear weapons are fundamentally different from conventional ones, a fact requiring no elaboration. A large part of the presently perceived threat of nuclear war arises from the desire of military planners to make nuclear weapons fulfill too many functions. In the early postwar years, when the United States had a monopoly, or at least supremacy, in nuclear weapons, they could be used as an atomic shield against a hypothetical invasion of Western Europe by the Soviet Union using conventional weapons. But in a world where both sides have approximately equal nuclear armaments, it is dangerous for either side to threaten the other with their use in order to deter conventional war. The height of irresponsibility in this matter was reached recently when L. W. Beilenson and S. T. Cohen, writing in the New York Times Magazine (March 14, 1982), advocated that we abandon our conventional armaments and rely entirely on nuclear weapons. They coupled this, in fact, with an appeal to return to isolationism.

Unfortunately, it is utopian to eliminate all wars in our time. Most of them are not even part of the great East-West conflict—for example, India versus Pakistan, Iraq versus Iran, Israel versus the Arabs. We cannot make the abolition of war or the good behavior of all nations on earth preconditions for dealing with the nuclear threat. The prime aim of the United States and the Soviets must be to prevent nuclear war by all means, and arms control agreements between the two superpowers, as well as self-restraint, are essential in doing it.

What kinds of arms control? The proposals are legion. One of the most attractive, initiated by George Kennan, would reduce the nuclear weapons on both sides by 50 percent *without negotiation*. This can be tolerated and is entirely compatible with the security of both superpowers. But this proposal is even better with the modification first suggested by Jeremy Stone of the Federation of American Scientists and then by Bob Bacher of the California Institute of Technology, namely: Let's go down 5 percent; let's scrap 5 percent of our nuclear weapons voluntarily and challenge the Soviets to do the same. We have sufficient intelligence capability to find out whether the Soviets actually do it. And if they follow us, let's make a second step and then a third step until we have reduced by 50 percent. In the meantime, let's negotiate a better treaty. But it is no use to postpone all action until a treaty can be negotiated. Whenever we try to do that, so many promises have to be made to our military that in fact an arms control treaty often amounts to a buildup. Although SALT II has kept a further buildup limited, the proposal to start reducing our armaments first and negotiate later is a good one. Then, even if the negotiations take five years or more, we would be no worse off.

Kenneth Waltz

We will not be able to control and limit nuclear weapons unless we ask ourselves earnestly—and keep asking ourselves—how we can use them most effectively for deterrent and for defensive purposes. War becomes more likely when a would-be attacker expects that he can attack at low cost, even if he fails, or that he can attack and easily succeed because of an inadequate defense thrown up against him.

How can we most effectively use nuclear weapons for defensive purposes? In the first place, nobody likes the *idea* of first use of nuclear weapons. You can ask almost anybody, "Are you in favor of first use?" and the answer will be no. But what are the alternatives? Winston Churchill once said, "No matter now absorbed generals become in playing their own games, they do occasionally have to consider what the adversary may do." We have to admit that Soviet doctrine and war-gaming indicate that if the Soviets were to move militarily, for example in Europe, it would be with combined conventional and nuclear arms. If we cannot devise ways of throwing up a conventional defense strong enough to stop such an attack, then we are forced to think seriously about first (or at least early) use of nuclear weapons.

The difficulty with what appears to be our present doctrine is that we contemplate using nuclear weapons at the moment—or just before the moment—of defeat. In other words, in the chaos of defeat we presumably will introduce nuclear weapons (the Soviets already having done so), and we will then almost inevitably use large ones, use them indiscriminately, and use them against deep targets as opposed to battlefield targets. One may deplore the early use of nuclear weapons, but also deplore their later use under such conditions. And these are the conditions we have to contemplate, because we live in a nuclear world.

Thus we see that it is not defensive or deterrent use that is good or bad, but rather how we plan to act defensively or how we plan to act in deterrent ways. Christoph Bertram rightly points out that the expectation of a miracle is not a good basis for military planning. It would indeed be expecting a miracle to think that by postponing the use of nuclear weapons we would reduce the possibility of their being used and increase the possibility of their being used in highly discriminate and very controlled ways.

Another point is that we have slipped—civilian and military commentators alike, private and public people alike—into thinking that nuclear weapons deter only nuclear weapons. They surely do that, but they also do more than that. For reasons understandable in terms of political and military interests and habits of thinking, we have gradually become persuaded that because of parity, or because of what some see as being our inferiority, nuclear deterrence no longer extends beyond our borders or covers conventional cases. That is an odd belief. In fact, as McGeorge Bundy knows better than anybody, it was in the middle 1960s, when we had reached a peak of numerical, strategic nuclear superiority, that we thought our nuclear deterrent did not provide enough deterrence. Then we dragged our NATO allies kicking and screaming behind us into a posture of flexible response. How odd that superiority, parity, and what some call inferiority all have had the same effect, causing us to think that we had to be able to act in a wide range of contingencies at a fairly high level of conventional competence!

This misconception misreads nuclear deterrence and misreads it in a way that is pleasing to certain political and military people because it indicates that we need ever more and more. That is, if we could contemplate (and many do) fighting a World War III that would be a World War II with nuclear weapons in the background, our fleet of 600 ships, as planned, is not nearly big enough. But if we cannot imagine fighting a major protracted war against the Soviet Union, in the nuclear age, in the presence of nuclear weapons, then much of the military buildup is not only misplaced but also counterproductive.

An earlier conception of deterrence holds that once you have secure second-strike weapons you have enough; you don't need more. You deter an adversary who threatens your vital interests, even if he does so only with conventional weapons, because he believes there is some risk that in threatening those vital interests he will cause you to retaliate. But he has to believe that there is that risk. He doesn't know what the probability is, but that doesn't matter. In threatening your vital interests, what could he gain that would be worth risking three cities? Or six cities? We don't have to talk about hundreds, or about one-third or one-half of the population, as Desmond Ball rightly points out.

By minimizing the extent to which deterrence deters, and the extent to which superiority, parity, and inferiority are irrelevant, we put ourselves in a position where we understandably begin to think that we need ever more and more. And we get ourselves into endless arms races— not only nuclear but also conventional ones. Unless we rethink our strategy, conventional *and* nuclear, we will continue to be in a position where noticeable and meaningful measures of arms control and disarmament are simply impossible.

Charles Wolf, Jr.

Before we look at the current situation in international security and arms control, we need to back up and think about how we got here. You will recall that the fundamental premise underlying détente in the 1970s was that a number of highly desirable consequences would result from weaving a web of relationships (in Henry Kissinger's artful and somewhat vulnerable metaphor) between the West and the East— economic relationships, arms control relationships, political relationships, cultural and scientific relationships. This web would contribute to moderating Soviet behavior abroad, perhaps to some loosening of the Soviet system at home, to the development of some degree of pluralism in Eastern Europe, and to the development of some degree of independence in the relationships between the countries of Eastern Europe and the Soviet Union.

In the 1980s, when we look at the record of the past decade, it is fair to say that by and large our European and Japanese allies see détente in a different light than we Americans do. (This is a drastic oversimplification. Certainly, many Europeans gravitate more to the view characterized as American, and perhaps many readers and most contributors to this book gravitate toward the view characterized as that of our allies.) Looking through different lenses, they see, for example, the development of Solidarity in Poland prior to December 13, 1981. They see the development of decentralized decision making via market socialism in the Hungarian economy. They see the development of a seemingly independent foreign policy in Romania. They see in particular the reuniting of some 200,000 German families formerly separated by the barriers between East and West Germany. Moreover, they see a faltering Soviet economy beset by declining rates of growth, declining productivity, repressed inflation, and labor shortages. They conclude that this is not as formidable an enemy, an adversary, as they had previously been willing to believe.

Through U.S. lenses, however, a different set of images appears. We see—or at least most of us see—a massive buildup of Soviet military forces, nuclear and conventional, air, naval, and ground. We see a rate of growth in Soviet military spending that has been more rapid than the rate of growth in the Soviet national product. We see a rate of military investment within the Soviet defense budget many times larger than our own. We see the repression of Solidarity after December 13, 1981, and the imposition of martial law in Poland. We see the invasion of Afghanistan. We see the tremendous expansion of the Soviet empire in Angola, in Ethiopia, South Yemen, Afghanistan, Southeast Asia, and elsewhere.

In sum, our European and Japanese friends—or many of them—conclude that détente and its premise of the web of relationships were valid in the 1970s and remain applicable in the 1980s. We—or many of us—conclude that détente and this underlying premise have been weighed in the balance and, like the kings of Babylon, found seriously wanting. We conclude further that the West's policies and relations toward the Soviet Union should be drastically altered over the spectrum of political relations, arms control negotiations, and economic relations.

This background is admittedly only a brief sketch of much more complex issues, but the fact that our main authors—especially Christoph Bertram and McGeorge Bundy—have failed to express or recognize it is unfortunate. This background conditions not only what is said here, but how we interpret what is said.

That Bertram is an eloquent representative and spokesman for the position characterized above as the European view is of course not surprising, but two points he makes are disturbing in the light of this background account of different evaluations placed on détente. He poses that Central America "is not an issue for international security unless the United States decides to make it one." Looking through one set of lenses, it seems that Central America would at least be *an* issue in international security considerations. *New York Times* reporter Allen Riding, who has been covering events in El Salvador, recently reported that the leaders of the five guerrilla groups in El Salvador told him that their efforts to oppose the Duarte regime were concerted by the Cuban offer to supply Soviet weapons last year. That is at least *an* issue in international security.

A second remarkable example of this perspective is Bertram's reference to the chronic instability in Eastern Europe, from which he goes on to forecast that crises as in Poland will occur more frequently in the coming decade, with the danger always present that Soviet military oppression will not succeed in limiting the conflict to one country, but that it might spread, possibly even spilling over into an East-West war. This is an eloquent and archetypical, as well as sobering, reflection of the viewpoint characterized earlier. In effect, he says that the success of Soviet military oppression in Eastern Europe is to be preferred to its failure, because the latter may ignite a war. If that becomes the dominant view in the West, and if those are the only two choices—that is, the success of Soviet military oppression or a war between East and West—the international security system will be fatally eroded and the decline of the West assured.

One point that Bundy and some of the other commentators—especially Desmond Ball—emphasized needs further examination. To the extent that there is a reduced role and reduced emphasis on nuclear forces and weapons, as we acknowledge there will be and ought to be, there needs to be greater emphasis placed on conventional forces in Europe and elsewhere, and on the development of a suitable counter to the Soviet's adroit use of surrogate or proxy forces. We tend to think of the range of forces as limited to our own and our Western allies' nuclear and conventional forces. We have no counter to the way the Soviets effectively use and motivate Cuban and East German combat, security, and police forces, giving them financial, logistic, communications, and intelligence support. The rapid deployment force is not an answer to that element. The use of European forces is not an answer. These are some of the issues that need to be addressed.

Part 2

Arms Control Policy and Prospects

3
Arms Control Policy
in the Reagan Administration

Robert Grey

The shadow of nuclear arms dominates world politics, and taming the nuclear weapon looms as one of the most fundamental problems in international affairs. This being the case, the arguments for major arms control efforts are compelling. Given the tense Soviet-U.S. relationship, if we are to be true to ourselves and responsible to the American people and to the world community at large, we must seek every opportunity to negotiate for peace, however adverse the odds may be.

In this respect, the Reagan administration, like every other U.S. administration since the beginning of the nuclear era, shares the commitment to limit nuclear armaments. Since the nuclear age began, U.S. policy has been guided by the conviction that the nuclear weapon must be abolished or at least brought under tight and effective control. By a fortuitous accident of history, we were the first country to have nuclear weapons. Then our moral concern made Americans wonder—as many still wonder—whether President Truman's use of the bomb was justified. Most Americans viewed, and continue to view, future use of nuclear weapons with revulsion.

In 1948, the United States proposed the Baruch Plan to bring its own monopoly of nuclear energy under international control. Since the Soviet Union's rejection of the plan—one of the decisive turning points of modern history—the United States has advanced one idea after another in a persistent search for a way to reduce the threat of nuclear war. Despite the failures and disappointments of that experience, the quest continues with greater urgency than ever, because the menace of nuclear weapons is far greater today than it was in the simpler time of the U.S. nuclear monopoly.

The United States remains committed to the proposition that the control of nuclear weapons is the key to the possibility of achieving a sustained and stable peace. In this perspective, peace must be defined as a dynamic process in which the behavior of states toward each other is governed by rules that are reciprocally accepted and reasonably well enforced. As we have all been reminded by the grim history of this century, peace is not the order of nature. It cannot be expected to survive without effective efforts to control the predatory instincts of man.

But arms control is not a thing apart; it does not exist in a vacuum. Those who urge this administration to do something or to be realistic about the horrifying implications of nuclear war—and I submit most emphatically that we are realistic about this—have an equal obligation to be realistic both about the nature of the Soviet Union, which is our principal antagonist in this area, and about the sustained buildup of the Soviet nuclear arsenal throughout the period when nuclear arms negotiations have been most vigorously pursued.

In the first place, the Soviet Union bears a heavy responsibility— indeed the primary responsibility—for much of the tension that has made it difficult to make real progress on nuclear arms reductions. We did not invade Czechoslovakia in 1968. We did not invade Afghanistan in 1979. We are not responsible for the tragic developments taking place today in Poland. And we are not providing the toxic weapons that are being used today in Cambodia, Laos, and Afghanistan. These weapons are being used, I might add, in flagrant violation of international treaties and of the fundamental tenets of international law. Simply put, thousands of innocent people have been murdered in a macabre experiment that can best be described as testing these ghastly products on the natives. Those who urge us to seek arms reductions without simultaneously rebuilding our own defenses, and who tend to dismiss our very real concerns about being certain that new arms control agreements can be effectively verifiable, should bear these tragic events in mind. We are not dealing with a like-minded society. We are dealing with a society based upon flawed ideological underpinnings that justify and condone practices that negate honorable behavior and fair dealing.

The Soviet military buildup is also alarming. At the time of the Cuban missile crisis, we had overwhelming nuclear superiority. But year after year since that time, our lead has been eroding; by the conclusion of the SALT I Treaty, the Soviets had caught up in several important categories and today possess a capability to destroy many of our land, sea, and air systems in a first strike. The relentless Soviet drive for a preeminent nuclear arsenal can be seen in the record of the past fifteen years:

- The Soviet strategic threat against the United States has increased fivefold.

- The Soviets have spent roughly three times more on strategic offensive forces than the United States has.

- The Soviet Union has developed and deployed its fourth generation of ICBMs. These include the SS-17, SS-18, and SS-19 ICBMs. These missiles deploy many more warheads, are far more powerful, and are just as accurate as the U.S. ICBMs.

- Three new Soviet submarine-launched ballistic missiles have been developed, and the most recent nuclear submarine, the Typhoon, has been deployed.

- The Soviet Backfire bomber, a bomber with intercontinental capabilities, is being deployed in large numbers.

- The world's most advanced strategic defense systems have been created to protect the Soviet Union from attack.

- A new generation of Soviet ICBMs, SLBMs, and ballistic missile submarines is under development, along with one or two new heavy bombers.

Some would argue that the Soviets were bound to draw more nearly even to us in the nuclear balance in any event, but it is equally clear that we have been less prudent in modernizing our own systems to ensure that we maintain a modern and viable deterrent capability. There has been no U.S.-Soviet nuclear arms race for the past fifteen years. Only the Soviets have been racing, and they appear to be seeking nuclear superiority.

So this administration believes it is imperative that our modernization program proceed if we are to restore our deterrent capability, which is the bedrock on which our national security, our foreign policy, and our hopes for attaining meaningful reductions in nuclear weapons on both sides rest.

It is worth recalling that the principal goal of U.S. nuclear weapons is to make certain that neither the Soviet Union nor any other country use or brandish nuclear weapons for aggressive purposes. To achieve this goal, the United States must at all times maintain a clear and visible second-strike capability, so that the United States, its allies, and its other vital interests can be protected against attack or the threat of attack, by whatever means may be required, across the full spectrum of possible threats. This is, and must remain, the minimal goal of our nuclear arsenal and is the ultimate guarantee of our freedom.

Our second goal is crisis stability, an essential element in the maintenance of peace. As we all know, the Soviet Union has chosen to put most of its nuclear power into land-based ICBMs, including several hundred extremely large missiles. Because of their number, their power, and their rapidly improving accuracy, Soviet ICBMs threaten the stability of deterrence. For this reason, our arms control efforts will necessarily focus on the issue of land-based missiles. This is our focus in the INF talks and will also be our focus in START. It is in our interest, in the interest of the Soviet Union, and in the interest of mankind that we structure any agreement—as well as our modernization program—to enhance confidence in the survivability of our second-strike forces, thereby reducing pressures to adopt launch-on-warning policies. In keeping with that concern, it is essential to achieve reductions in those Soviet ICBMs that threaten the survivability of our land-based ICBMs and other strategic forces. We must also achieve reductions in the Soviet mobile SS-20s and other missiles that constitute a major threat to Europe, Japan, China, and the Middle East.

Our third goal in arms control is to enhance the security of our alliance. Western European security is being threatened by the Soviet buildup of SS-20 launchers, which now number over three hundred, most of which can reach all parts of Western Europe. These missiles are particularly threatening, as they have three accurate, independently targetable warheads. Concern over Soviet development of these inter-mediate-range nuclear weapons led the West about five years ago to examine what steps needed to be taken to deter the use of Soviet intermediate-range ballistic missiles. The result of this concern was the NATO decision of 1979 that the United States deploy its own intermediate-range, land-based missiles in Europe while at the same time negotiating with the Soviet Union about removing the threat to Europe caused by Soviet missiles. This allied decision, an integral component of Western security strategy, is being carried out today through our Pershing II and ground-launched cruise missile deployment decisions on the one hand and the INF arms control negotiations on the other.

Arms control efforts in the past have been deeply disappointing. Instead of fulfilling our high expectations, past strategic offensive arms control agreements have done no more than codify existing levels of arms. This failure, in large measure, has to do with the very different objectives that the United States and the Soviet Union have pursued in arms control. In SALT I, the Soviet objective was an ABM Treaty to deny the United States the military advantage of its lead in ABM research and development; the U.S. objective was to control defenses in order to set agreed and stabilizing limits on the growth and improvement of the Soviet and the U.S. strategic offensive arsenals, so that each side could maintain a deterrent position. The SALT I agreements failed to accomplish the U.S. objective.

In 1972, we were greatly concerned over the prospect of a major Soviet nuclear arms buildup and formally announced that if the SALT process failed within five years to produce a more thorough agreement equitably limiting strategic offensive arms, "the supreme interests of the

United States" could be jeopardized, establishing grounds for withdrawal from the ABM Treaty. Congress later confirmed this position.

The simple fact of the matter is that what we most feared in 1972 took place. The terms, the loopholes, and the ambiguities of the 1972 Interim Agreement on the Limitation of Strategic Offensive Arms permitted the Soviet Union to forge ahead in its strategic arms buildup while the United States rested on its oars. The strategic stability the United States sought through SALT I proved to be a chimera. The Soviet Union took full advantage of a combination of political and military circumstances that favored its plans for expansion: the uncertainties of the U.S. mood in the aftermath of Vietnam; the Soviet attainment of strategic nuclear equality and corresponding changes in the relative level of conventional and theater nuclear forces; and, above all, the U.S. attitudes that flowed from our assumption that the Soviet Union shared our interest in parity, mutual deterrence, and peace.

These adverse trends were accentuated during the long period while the United States and the Soviet Union negotiated the SALT II Treaty, and the U.S. Senate then debated the merits of the treaty and refused to ratify it. We must learn from the mistakes of the past, or we shall surely repeat them. It is at least arguable that the unit of account used in SALT II might have addressed the problems we faced in the late 1960s but doesn't suffice for the situation we face today. Rather than achieving more stable forces at lower levels, the SALT II Treaty would have permitted a continued massive buildup in Soviet destructive capability, relegated the United States to a position of permanent nuclear inferiority, and undercut the nuclear deterrent that has protected Western Europe, Japan, and other vital interests of the United States since 1945.

It is, therefore, not surprising, that out of frustration with the past arms control process there has emerged a grass-roots proposal calling for a freeze on nuclear weapons. The Hatfield-Kennedy resolution called upon the United States and the Soviet Union to halt immediately the production, testing, and deployment of all nuclear weapons. This moratorium would be followed by efforts to reduce the nuclear arsenals of both sides.

The freeze proposal is a product of the genuine concern among Americans over the danger of nuclear war. This is a natural concern, spurred by the perception of a world situation characterized by increasing danger. But a nuclear freeze, while conceived with the best of intentions, would not be a sound or effective basis for achieving the far-reaching arms control objectives we have set out for ourselves, in particular greater stability through substantial reductions in the nuclear capabilities of both sides to equal levels. A freeze would seriously undercut the prospects of achieving reductions by removing Soviet incentives to negotiate in earnest on substantial arms reductions. The strategic modernization program announced by President Reagan in October 1981, designed to reverse adverse trends in the strategic balance, provides the best incentive for the Soviets to consider and accept significant mutual reductions through effective, verifiable arms control agreements. Because a freeze would preclude the U.S. modernization program, it is not in our security interests and would deprive the United States of essential negotiating leverage.

A freeze would codify an unstable and worrisome strategic situation. While the United States exercised substantial unilateral restraint during the past decade, the Soviets' across-the-board modernization efforts have resulted in serious U.S. vulnerabilities, especially the vulnerability of virtually our entire ICBM force to a preemptive Soviet strike. By blocking critical modernization programs designed to restore the credibility of U.S. deterrent forces, a freeze would prevent us from rectifying present vulnerabilities.

A freeze would also damage Western Alliance security and arms control objectives. The destabilizing consequences of the Soviet military buildup are understood by our NATO allies, and they strongly support our modernization programs as essential to correcting existing imbalances and promoting a stable deterrent that ensures both U.S. and European security. As we have embarked on the very important INF negotiations with the Soviet Union in Geneva, the United States and the NATO allies must preserve the two-track modernization and arms control approach that NATO endorsed in 1979. A freeze proposal at current levels would concede to the USSR their present nuclear advantage in Europe and would eliminate any Soviet incentive to reach a fair and balanced agreement that would reduce INF missiles to zero.

The president and the administration share the concern felt throughout the world of the danger that nuclear weapons pose for mankind. That is why the president has proposed a far-reaching arms control program for seeking equitable and verifiable agreements, which will not only freeze current nuclear and conventional forces but actually significantly reduce them.

A freeze would not only deal with the deployment of nuclear delivery systems. It would also ban the testing of nuclear weapons. For over two decades, under leaders from both parties, the United States has recognized a comprehensive nuclear test ban (CTB) to be an important objective in the arms control process. The United States continues to view a CTB as a desirable long-term goal. But we believe that, under present circumstances, the threat posed by nuclear weapons can best be reduced through arms control measures such as those we are now pursuing—that is, through negotiations aimed at producing deep reductions in intermediate-range and strategic nuclear weapons and at achieving a more stable military balance.

While we do not believe that this is a propitious time for action on a comprehensive test ban, we have not lost interest in seeking solutions to problems that must be solved before any CTB is possible. Foremost of these is the long-standing problem of verification. In this area, the United States looks forward to cooperating with members of the Geneva Committee on Disarmament in discussing questions that relate to verification of a CTB.

In Geneva, the United States is negotiating as well with the Soviet Union on the basis of the president's bold zero-level proposal, which calls for the elimination of the Soviet nuclear systems most threatening to Europe in exchange for cancellation of scheduled NATO deployments of intermediate-range, land-based nuclear missiles. In these very important INF negotiations, the United States is seeking far more than a freeze. Our goal in Geneva is the elimination of the more threatening land-based missiles.

In short, the Reagan administration is committed to going well beyond what has been achieved so far in the field of arms control—well beyond the mere codification of both sides' military posture plans. We now have a historic opportunity to make a new and more promising beginning— an opportunity to make real progress in controlling nuclear weapons and reducing the risk of nuclear war. But the best way to embark on this vital task is not to freeze present capabilities. It is to proceed with our essential modernization programs, while at the same time vigorously and persistently negotiating agreements that, for the first time, would promote real stability at much lower levels of armaments.

Any agreement on significant reductions in nuclear weapons must have sound provisions on verification. Effective verification is an absolute prerequisite for any treaty. One example that comes to mind regarding compliance and verification concerns the use of chemical warfare in Asia by signatories of international agreements against its use. This should remind us of the fragility of arms control agreements and the absence of good faith currently being demonstrated. A START agreement cannot simply be based on taking the Soviets' word that they will adhere to the terms of the treaty. Considerably tighter verification provisions and procedures than agreed upon previously will be essential. In the past, national technical means of verification were considered sufficient. In a START agreement, we will insist on whatever cooperative measures are necessary to monitor the terms of the agreement regarding destructive potential.

For the entire period of the nuclear age, this nation has been successful in devising a national security and foreign policy based upon nuclear deterrence and a system of alliances with like-minded nations. The system, which has enjoyed broad bipartisan support, has been severely tested, most notably in Korea and in Vietnam, but it has endured. As a result of our efforts and the efforts of others, we have seen a developing world society adjust to the emergence of a vast number of new states, a world in which the respect for the independence and dignity both of societies and individuals has made significant advances. This is not to say there is not a great deal left to be done. Where there is hunger, injustice, and violence there will always be a great deal to be done; but on the whole we have been successful. No nuclear weapons have been used for almost forty years.

These policies, even tested as they are by time, are still relatively new and not entirely congenial to the American people, whose historical instincts still tug them away from involvement in the world beyond our shores. We ought to bear this in mind as we prepare once again to negotiate limits on nuclear weapons. There are no simple solutions or unilateral initiatives that can put the genie back in the bottle. Success will come only through sustained and difficult negotiations with an ideological adversary who is regrettably still in the imperial mode. To succeed in these negotiations, we have to make it clear that this generation of Americans, like those before, is willing to make the sacrifices necessary to obtain the peace with freedom and security.

We are a great and an idealistic people, but occasionally in the body politic there surfaces a movement that embodies a naive utopianism; this is the vulnerable side of U.S. idealism. We cannot wish away our problems by ignoring the international environment in which we must conduct foreign policy. We tried that twice in the past, and we paid for it dearly. William Manchester's brilliant book *Goodbye Darkness* recounts the incredible sacrifices that ill-equipped and underprepared young Americans and Australians made against very difficult odds in stemming the Japanese advance toward Sydney and San Francisco. These efforts would not have been necessary if we had had the foresight to build credible defenses backed by a prudent foreign policy. This is the unmistakable lesson of history, which we ignore at our peril.

It has been argued in West Germany that some among us are unable to see the difference between the authority of democracy and that of a dictatorship. Emotionalism is equated with morality; if you're reasonable, you're immoral, some argue. But in spite of such emotional spasms, the administration remains optimistic and confident that when put to the test our people and those of our allied governments will support the arms control proposals of the administration, as well as the defense and diplomatic policies essential to sustain them.

4
Beginning Nuclear Disarmament at the Bottom

Herbert F. York

Nuclear disarmament is both a goal and a process. The *goal* of nuclear disarmament, utopian at present, is the complete elimination of nuclear weapons. The *process* of nuclear disarmament consists of those actions and policies that move the world toward that goal. Elements of such a process would include major reductions (i.e., greater than 50 percent) in weapons overall, the elimination of certain types of nuclear weapons, and the elimination of nuclear weapons from certain specific areas, either totally or by major types. The purpose of complete nuclear disarmament is to eliminate the possibility of nuclear war altogether; the purpose of the various partial measures constituting the elements of the process is to eliminate or substantially reduce the possibility of nuclear wars of certain types or in certain places and to advance the total process toward the ultimate goal.

Nuclear arms control, on the other hand, is quite different in both its elements and its purposes. Essentially, nuclear arms control is a process for managing the arms race and includes such items as numerical ceilings, small reductions in numbers, and hot-line arrangements. Among its purposes are: to reduce the probability of war in general by contributing to strategic and political stability; to set a limitation on total destructive potential; and to hold down overall arms spending. While these purposes are good, there are better ways than nuclear arms control for achieving every one of them. One additional purpose of nuclear arms control, however, is to build the necessary basis from which it will become possible to launch the process of nuclear disarmament. For those who believe, as I do, that nuclear war is, and ought to remain, sharply distinguishable from conventional war and that nuclear war poses a singularly grave danger to mankind and to civilization, it is this last purpose of nuclear arms control that is of the greatest importance.

With these definitions and purposes in mind, I propose to examine a particular possibility for beginning the nuclear disarmament process at the bottom rather than at the top—that is, by beginning with the elimination of battlefield nuclear weapons rather than with the elimination or substantial reduction of strategic nuclear weapons. By battlefield nuclear weapons I mean those intended for use right in the battle zone itself, certainly including nuclear artillery and missiles of similar range and perhaps of somewhat longer ranges as well.

The attempt to seriously reduce strategic nuclear weapons has been stymied for some time. The reasons are connected with the uniquely enormous destructive and killing power of these very large weapons and include such specifics as (1) the fear that a substantial reduction in numbers would create a situation in which we could not accomplish the objectives of our nuclear strategies, (2) the fear that the kind of cheating that could escape the existing verification system could result in a decisive advantage to our antagonists, and (3) the fact that the two superpowers intend to keep membership in the superpower club restricted to themselves alone, which in turn means that there is a floor under their forces that is several, or even many, times the size of the force of nuclear power number three, be that Britain, France, or China. Battlefield nuclear weapons do not play a similarly unique role. Their purposes include stopping tanks (by killing or incapacitating their crews) and destroying other relatively small military targets on a battlefield, and there are alternative conventional (meaning nonnuclear) means for accomplishing these same objectives. Indeed many believe that these conventional alternatives are superior to nuclear battlefield weapons, especially when one takes into account the military realities associated with the political difficulties inherent in obtaining permission to release nuclear weapons for use. For these and other reasons, the questions and problems associated with the elimination of battlefield nuclear weapons are very different from those associated with major reductions in strategic weapons. We can hope that moving in this new direction will result in avoiding the problems that have so severely inhibited progress in START.

Scope and Form of the Limitation

Ideally, the elimination of battlefield weapons should include the destruction of all of them everywhere. However, in light of the balance between the benefits and costs of their elimination, it would be better for us in the United States and for the world if we were the only ones to do it. Such an action is not as "unbalanced" as it may seem, because we alone introduced these weapons into Europe two decades ago, and even today a large majority of those deployed in Central Europe are ours.

Of course, the elimination of battlefield nuclear weapons should not be done precipitously or in any way that would create sudden changes in the military balances. Compensating changes in the conventional forces would have to take place concurrently, and this would require some time. However, the record of progress in nuclear arms control and disarmament shows that it has never taken place too rapidly. The problem has always been that it scarcely takes place at all.

It would be best to eliminate battlefield nuclear weapons on a multilateral basis, which could be done either with or without a treaty to back up the process. In the case of weapons widely recognized as potentially more dangerous and troublesome than they are worth—such as bacteriological weapons—a simple declaration to eschew their use has been deemed sufficient. But in the case of battlefield nuclear weapons, political considerations may make it necessary to negotiate a treaty that includes verification provisions. If so, the problem becomes more complex because there is no verification system adequate to monitor the total elimination of such easily transported weapons.

Thus the nature of the proposed elimination would have to be substantially modified to bring adequate verification within reach. This could be done by narrowing the geographic scope of the action while simultaneously broadening it to include restrictions that would result in more easily detected "observables." The geographic scope might, therefore, be the zone included within, say, one hundred miles on both sides of the inter-German border, or, better, all of both Germanys plus Czechoslovakia. The added restrictions would then include a prohibition on storing nuclear weapons of any kind in that zone, elimination of all nuclear storage facilities in the zone, and a prohibition on the conduct of large-scale exercises that imply the use of battlefield nuclear weapons.

Such a combination of restrictions would make it impossible to store other longer-range nuclear weapon systems in the zone as well. This measure by itself would not prevent those weapons from fulfilling their military or deterrent functions because they could be operated from bases in Europe outside the zone or from the nearby seas. This is assuming that such longer-range weapons were not themselves eliminated by some other agreement.

The Benefits and Costs of Eliminating Battlefield Nuclear Weapons

The principal benefit of this proposed action is that it would substantially raise the nuclear threshold. It would make it less probable

GOSHEN COLLEGE LIBRARY
GOSHEN, INDIANA

that a conventional action in Europe by the Soviets, of whatever size and scope, would be met with a nuclear response that could easily set off a full-scale nuclear war. Indeed, the main argument in support of deploying battlefield nuclear weapons, including the so-called neutron bomb, is that they make a nuclear response to a conventional attack more likely and therefore more credible. Thus, theoretically, their mere presence enhances deterrence.

Those who see little or no difference between nuclear war and conventional war regard this as a good thing, while those of us who believe there is a great difference see it as a very bad thing. To us, a combination of military strategy and hardware deployment that achieves deterrence in such a way that any failure in that deterrence leads to the total destruction of Europe "in order to save it" is a military situation to be eliminated, not further enhanced.

A second potential benefit, probably of comparable importance, derives from the fact that nuclear weapons—nuclear battlefield weapons in particular—are the opiate of the defense planners, both in Washington and in Europe. In Europe, this problem takes the form of overreliance on nuclear weapons for maintaining deterrence and further overreliance on the United States as the principal developer, provider, and controller of nuclear weapons. In Washington, the problem takes the form of inadequate attention to, and resources for, the production, deployment, and development of conventional alternatives (precision-guided munitions, cluster munitions, improved C^3I, and the like). The presence of so many nuclear weapons in the hands of NATO has for years allowed NATO officials, Americans included, to avoid doing whatever must be done in order to prepare to defend Europe without totally destroying it in the process.

A third potential benefit is that some of the resources necessary for making the adjustments and improvements needed to provide for an adequate conventional defense can be found in the financial and personnel savings that would result from the elimination of battlefield nuclear weapons in Europe. A large number of U.S. troops and many physical and financial resources go into the protection of nuclear weapons and the maintenance of the special and largely separate command and logistics systems that back them up. The elimination of nuclear battlefield systems would free up some of these resources, as would the redeployment of other longer-range nuclear systems to areas removed from the battle zone.

Counterposed against the above benefits are the benefits that the deployment of battlefield weapons in Europe supposedly brings. In effect, not receiving these purported benefits would become the cost of eliminating battlefield nuclear weapons.

First, there is the idea that the deployment of nuclear weapons in Europe serves to couple NATO's conventional forces in Europe to the U.S. strategic forces in North America and at sea. This is the concept of the "NATO triad." It is claimed that the deployment of battlefield nuclear weapons in particular makes this "coupling" more credible. However, it must be submitted that it is the enormous killing power of the larger nuclear weapons that frightens political leaders and thus forms the basis of the enormous political influence of nuclear weapons and of their role in both deterrence and self-deterrence. The notion that the presence of the much smaller battlefield weapons significantly adds to this is an elaboration that appeals to theorists but has little basis in practical political reality—and none at all in experience.

A second purported benefit in deploying battlefield nuclear weapons, nuclear artillery in particular, is that should deterrence fail, these weapons could be used effectively to blunt and contain a massive armor attack from the east. Counterposed against this notion are three factors:

- Even the limited use of battlefield nuclear weapons is likely to lead to the use of larger weapons and thus to all-out nuclear war, an event that most of us believe must not happen.

- It is unlikely that permission to release battlefield nuclear weapons would be given in a timely fashion, if at all. Under such a circumstance, these weapons alone could not contribute to containing the attack, and adequate numbers and types of conventional weapons will not be available, in part because of the high opportunity costs incurred in providing nuclear weapons.

- Even if we overlook the undesirability of using battlefield nuclear weapons and also assume permission to use them is obtained, there is still no reason to believe it would benefit us to use them, even considered solely within a military context.

Nuclear proponents often say that "we cannot stop a massive armored assault in Central Europe without the use of nuclear weapons," thus implying that we could with their use. However, there is no solid basis for believing this is true. If only the defenders had nuclear weapons they would indeed produce a military advantage, but this has not been the case for a long time, and there is absolutely no experiential basis or good theoretical basis for believing that their use confers an advantage on the defender in the real world, where both sides have large numbers of nuclear weapons in a wide variety of forms and with powers measured in megatons.

The third benefit that is said to derive from the deployment of battlefield nuclear weapons is that their mere presence near the battlefront causes all forces, armor included, to disperse, and that such a circumstance favors the defense. Although the tactical details of this point can be argued, it is likely that modern technology could produce an analogous situation without involving nuclear weapons. Other types of area munitions, cluster munitions containing smart or semismart submunitions and the like, are possible and would become available relatively soon if the large opportunity costs inherent in battlefield nuclear forces were diverted to the development and deployment of such conventional weapons.

Verification

A verification system consists of a complex of people, hardware, treaty clauses, and procedures and is supposed to fulfill two basic purposes in connection with arms control or disarmament treaties:

1. To deter the parties to a treaty from violating it in any way, by making the risk of being caught greater than the value of that particular violation, including very small ones.

2. To make certain major violations, or a large number of smaller violations of the kind that could create a significant change in the military balance, are detected in time for the necessary counteraction to be undertaken.

The first of these purposes gives rise to some requirements for the verification system that are relative to the particular violation they are designed to expose. The second gives rise to certain absolute requirements. Let us examine how purposes and requirements relate to verifying a treaty covering the removal of battlefield nuclear weapons from a "free" zone in Central Europe.

The way these weapons are intended to be used means that a substantial capability requires that there be thousands of them, that they be dispersed all along the projected front, that they be stored close to the delivery systems that employ them, and that they be in the hands of many tens of thousands of troops and officers who were trained in large-scale exercises that assumed the use of such weapons and who were also trained to cope with the effects of their use by the enemy. The verification system, therefore, needs to have an absolute capability of promptly detecting a violation on the scale of the re-creation or continuation of a nuclear capability comparable to that which currently exists.

On the other hand, the re-creation (or continuation) of a nuclear capability consisting of only a few (or even a hundred) battlefield nuclear weapons stored in several widely separated, secret locations and in the hands of a small cadre of specialists trained in an area remote from those we can easily observe would not significantly change the military balance. Therefore, the performance requirements of the verification system need only be matched to such deployments in the relative degree described above.

To understand the difference between this situation and that inherent in SALT, consider the extreme case of total elimination of strategic nuclear weapons. In such a case, the reintroduction, or retention, by just one side of a handful of multimegaton weapons would gravely affect the balance of power. The verification system would therefore have to be able to detect small numbers of such weapons stored in only one or a few sites in remote places and in the hands of a small cadre of persons expert in their use. The contrast between these two situations makes it clear that we cannot simply take over the ideas about verification developed in the SALT context and apply them directly to the generation of a treaty eliminating nuclear artillery and other similar systems.

An additional feature of beginning the nuclear disarmament process at the bottom is the obvious implication that a violation of an agreement to eliminate small short-range nuclear weapons would automatically bring nuclear weapons of the next larger size and range into play in some form (diplomatic, political, or military). The equivalent implication does not exist in the case of beginning the process at the top, with strategic weapons.

In sum, beginning the nuclear disarmament process at the bottom would be clearly beneficial. It would differ from previous attempts in such a way that we would have to rethink the entire process, and in doing so we might well be able to break through the logjam of fears and problems that have prevented further progress in this literally vital area for so long.

Discussion of Part 2

Richard Betts

Debates among various proponents of arms control tend to be theological in character because we have no historical experience or evidence about large-scale nuclear war to guide us. We all know that nuclear war would be an unprecedented horror, but no one knows how counterforce exchanges would unfold. These are the questions that tend to drive actual arms control bargaining and negotiations.

Different schools of thought focus on different variables in the complex structure of the military balance and base their arguments on different assumptions about which variables should have more weight. These assumptions can be disputed by arguments based on logical deduction but cannot be disproved by empirical tests. It is, of course, a good thing that we can't test propositions about how a nuclear engagement might unfold and which elements of weaponry would prove most significant. Because our judgments must be made on the basis of abstract analysis, debates on nuclear balance and the desirable formulations for limiting or constraining forces through negotiations often turn into dialogues of the deaf, with different schools ignoring basic parts of the others' frames of reference.

As for the purposes of arms control and the standards for judging it, let us start with four basic propositions. First, the only logical goal of serious nuclear arms control is to establish parity or equality between both sides so that neither has an overall advantage in the size and capability of its forces. Without parity, arms control may be irrelevant because it is possible for both the United States and the Soviet Union to unilaterally establish secure second-strike capabilities. If we accept the simple theory of mutual assured destruction as an adequate basis for a policy, arms control becomes unnecessary because assured destruction poses *absolute* requirements for retaliatory forces, not *relative* requirements (as does a counterforce strategy). Equality is a relative concept, not an absolute one.

The second proposition is that if arms control is necessary, and parity in nuclear weapons is a goal, success in that enterprise will not save money unless we are willing to accept higher risk by reducing our overall capabilities (including options for nuclear escalation) to contain a Soviet attack on Western Europe with conventional forces, or unless we are able to induce the Soviets to reduce their conventional forces to a degree much greater than we have any evidence to date that they would consider.

Third, reductions in nuclear weapons are desirable, but only if the pattern of reduction does not reduce the stability of mutual Soviet-U.S. deterrence. Under some conditions, reduced reliance on nuclear weapons could raise the danger of war breaking out.

Fourth, the United States and its allies could have reduced reliance on nuclear weapons long ago were it not for one basic problem. The U.S. and Western European publics don't want to pay the price—financially and in social terms—for the alternative. Nuclear weapons have been preferred as the bedrock of our deterrent force because they are cheaper than alternative instruments of military deterrence: specifically, conventional forces. Strategic nuclear forces account for less than 20 percent of the U.S. defense budget. But given the contingencies we have most reason to worry about, our nuclear forces are probably the least important part of our military forces.

Arms control, of course, is not an end in itself but only a means of increasing our security and making us safer. Thus, if Ambassador Herbert York's foregoing proposal is to be favored, it must not be simply because it would have a greater chance of being negotiable than other sorts of arms control, but because it would make the NATO central front more stable. On the other hand, if the Reagan administration's proposals for arms control initiatives are favored, it must be because unilateral military buildup by the United States is feasible and will buttress security and stability better than arms control, or because more modest positions than the United States is reportedly advancing would lead to agreements that would reduce our security. From all reports, the negotiating positions the administration is maintaining are, without a doubt, miles away from being negotiable with the Soviet Union.

Two questions must be asked about any arms control agreement: Is arms control fair in terms of being equal? And, Will we be better off with it or without it in terms of relative military capabilities? There is a dangerous tendency to confuse the answers to these questions. On SALT II, for example, it was possible for President Reagan and his advisers and a large sector of the defense community to argue that the treaty was inequitable. However, with realistic views of the alternatives, it was not possible to argue that our military power vis-à-vis the USSR would be stronger without the treaty. During the term of that treaty, major U.S. programs such as the MX missile, the Trident submarine, the B-1 or STEALTH bombers, or any other major improvement in our capabilities would be basically unconstrained. The Soviets, meanwhile, would have had to dismantle 10 percent of their launchers and restrain the capability most worrisome to the United States—their vast counterforce capability in intercontinental ballistic missiles—by limiting the warhead fractionation (that is, the number of warheads they could put on each missile) to a maximum of ten.

A different view of the problem is suggested by a proposal to eliminate battlefield nuclear weapons. Doing so could be both equitable and advantageous if the net overall military balance that has maintained relative stability in Europe for many years is not disrupted in the bargain. As Ambassador York has said, it would require improving NATO conventional defenses to compensate. However, the proposal is a possibility that appears unlikely to be fulfilled in the future, as it has been, with the brief exception of the mid-1960s, in the past. Technical fixes, such as increased reliance on precision-guided munitions, are an illusory solution. Although they would help, they don't clearly and uniquely favor the defense as much as some common views have recently maintained. The only way to eliminate battlefield nuclear weapons with much confidence is to raise new ground force divisions and deploy more artillery and tanks—and that means spending more money than battlefield tactical nuclear weapons cost.

This brings us to one of the basic dilemmas that bedevils nuclear arms control. Limits on one category of forces may not be helpful unless matched by limits on other categories. Nuclear weapons are only one part of a military balance that reinforces deterrence and stability. Since 1945, military stability in Europe has been viewed in the West as resting on countervailing superiorities—Soviet conventional superiority versus U.S. nuclear superiority, which theoretically underwrote the threat of retaliatory escalation, that is, first use of nuclear weapons if NATO conventional defenses buckled.

As the Soviets achieved nuclear parity, there was interest in codifying the nuclear balance in SALT. To do so without suffering a net decline in the relative Western military position, SALT treaties would logically have had to be linked with a mutual balanced force reduction (MBFR) agreement. This did not happen because the Soviet unwillingness to unilaterally reduce conventional capabilities was not matched by Western democracies' willingness to increase their own conventional capabilities—at least to the same extent. This disparity was cushioned in the early 1970s by détente. There was the hope that the significant decline in tension between the blocs would reduce the risks of a modest decline in the Western military position.

Today the cushion of détente, at least from this side of the Atlantic, seems to be gone. Yet there is only slightly greater willingness to match Soviet capabilities on all levels, strategic and theater nuclear forces as well as conventional forces, as West German Chancellor Helmut Schmidt recommended in his 1977 speech. The very political viability of the NATO alliance has even come into question. In this context, Ambassador York's proposal on battlefield tactical nuclear weapons may be unobjectionable, although the verification problems are more difficult than he allows. But in a general sense, it may be incidental compared to the other issues in military balance and arms control facing us. Furthermore, there is no clear evidence that agreement between the superpowers on battlefield tactical nuclear weapons would be any easier to reach than agreement on any other aspect of military capabilities.

The Reagan administration is possibly getting us into the worst of both worlds by sharply increasing the provocation of Moscow and at the same time offering only modest improvements in capabilities relevant to Europe and the central strategic balance—the areas that dominate the arms control agenda. The biggest military improvements in the Reagan defense program involve the navy, which would not appreciably reduce relative Soviet capability for overrunning Europe in a war or for waging a nuclear war. If there is not a major compromise in the administration's negotiating proposal—for example, in the theater nuclear force negotiation, in some tacit form or other, taking account of British and French forces—we may wind up acting in the reverse of Teddy Roosevelt's dictum, that is, "speaking stickly and carrying a big soft."

However, greater realism by the administration will not suffice if Western publics fail to face up to their real choices. If we want to reduce reliance on nuclear weapons, we will have to spend more, rather than less, money on defense, unless we can induce the Soviets to negotiate reductions in conventional forces, or unless we are willing to take higher risks and rely on the benevolence of Soviet intentions. We may need to reconsider our commitments to maintain capabilities for defending Western Europe with high confidence.

Finally, few of those activists supporting a nuclear freeze—however that term would be defined operationally if it were accepted—are likely to endorse what seems like the logical corollary: for instance, a return to conscription and higher spending to replace some of the reliance on nuclear weapons with better nonnuclear defenses. Unless those proponents are willing to take a basic position of pacifism and admit relative unconcern with the need for deterrence, they are being as unrealistic as the Reagan administration, and the chances for any meaningful arms control, which are already quite slim, will be nil.

Michael May

Arms control, as a means of reaching peace, is going to have to work with the world pretty much the way it is now. Although our institutions may need to be radically restructured, such restructuring lacks political support and, more important, guidelines. A world where linkage between nuclear and nonnuclear issues exists, however distasteful or complicated, is inevitable. In fact, linkage is possibly the major factor in the problem of relations between the United States and the Soviet Union. It would be far easier to maintain stable relations if we both existed with only the nuclear standoff issue.

Arms control must contribute to peace in a world where conventional war in such critical areas as Europe is virtually as dangerous as nuclear war because it is certain to lead to nuclear war. It is impossible to conceive of any conventional war in Europe that would not have disastrous consequences. At the same time, arms control in the 1980s must take into consideration the unsatisfactory, possibly fragile, and certainly not permanent tools that have been developed in the last thirty years to maintain general peace.

One major example is a largely invulnerable weapon system designed to counterbalance the advantage that would necessarily fall to an attacker in a nuclear exchange. Nuclear weapons cannot be uninvented; they cannot be erased from human knowledge or consciousness. Therefore, the next best solution is a weapon system that will make the difference between a first-strike and a response as small as possible. Arms control must provide for that; it must also accommodate the sharp and clearly recognized line in Europe, which was drawn in the immediate aftermath of World War II. That line was, of course, a tragic proposition, leaving many millions of people living on the side they would rather not live on. Nevertheless, the line established between U.S. forces on one side and Soviet forces on the other, both armed with nuclear weapons, has served to replace the centuries-old breeding ground of war in Europe with an arrangement that so far has allayed the causes that led to those wars.

No one knows if that will continue, but arms control in the 1980s must support the existence and preservation of this line in Europe. Arms control must also fit in with other existing policies that have served to maintain the peace. Primary among them is our alliance with Japan, without which the problems in Asia might be considerably worse. Arms control will have to work with the relationship we are developing with

China, which is a cautious modus vivendi. At present these areas are not directly impinged upon by arms control proposals, but they will have to be considered in the course of time.

Herbert York has stated his opinion that nuclear disarmament would eliminate the possibility of nuclear war. However, even if disarmament were possible, it would do no such thing because nuclear weapons can be built again; they can be built in periods of tension, and they can be recreated by thousands if not hundreds of thousands of people around the world. There is nothing we can do about it.

Concerning York's statement that disarmament should start at the bottom, two points must be made. Although the short-range battlefield nuclear weapons in Europe should not be viewed as a panacea, they do reinforce the line that has been drawn there. They help remind both the Soviet Union and us that whatever we may say about each other's actions, very little is likely to happen. To the degree that tactical nuclear weapons contribute to this state of affairs, we would eliminate them at some peril. As mentioned earlier, allowing a conventional rather than nuclear war in Europe is not an alternative. The kind of dangerous political situation that would permit a conventional war would undoubtedly lead to further cataclysm.

Another objection to the proposal of starting disarmament at the bottom is that this is not where the major problems are. The battlefield weapons in Europe do not threaten Moscow directly. They do threaten the Soviets in case they initiate European war, but they are no cause of panic in Moscow. The same cannot be said of weapons like the Pershing II, which combine a very short warning time to the Soviet Union with an excessive degree of vulnerability. A more effective place for disarmament to start in Europe would be in the intermediate-range nuclear forces, including forces like the Pershing II and comparable Soviet missiles.

As Robert Grey has stated, there are no simple solutions that are going to put the nuclear genie back in the bottle. Arms control does not exist in a vacuum, and the three goals he outlined for arms control policy for the United States, goals that have been largely shared by previous administrations, are essentially correct: to maintain clear and visible second-strike capability, to try to maintain crisis stability, and to enhance confidence in the alliance.

Arms control is considerably less disappointing if we look at it from the viewpoint of human history over the centuries. Perhaps SALT II was not so bad (although this is an opinion biased by my personal participation in SALT II). There are shortcomings in SALT II, particularly in the units of account—launchers for nuclear weapons—which are not the right units of account. But SALT II did introduce some other units of account. It introduced throwweight; it put some (admittedly high) limits on throwweight. It introduced overall missile weight as a unit of account. It was a step in the right direction, although we have a long way to go. Negotiations that take further steps toward installing the right units of account—namely, the ones that actually measure destructive power—would be most welcome.

To do this, improvements must be made in our verification procedures, and agreed cooperative measures must be developed with the Soviet Union to make these better units of account—presumably missiles—verifiable. Once again, the fact that such agreement did not take place at SALT II doesn't mean that SALT II was completely disappointing. Another welcome development would be to lower the overall totals, which are very high. They are higher than we would have liked to see them at SALT II and higher, of course, than the United States proposed. Any progress made in this direction by the administration is going to be welcomed by everyone.

The prospect for arms control in the 1980s depends on our ability to maintain political equilibrium in the crucial areas of the world and that equilibrium is going to have to adjust to political and socioeconomic changes as they occur. We must work to enhance and strengthen the basic policies mentioned earlier, such as the maintenance of adequately survivable strategic forces, although the present situation is not one of dire distress. We have to remedy some vulnerabilities, but on the whole, strategic imbalance is not the main concern at this time. We must maintain the situation in Europe so that the necessary political evolution that takes place, particularly on the eastern side of the Iron Curtain, does not lead to the kind of acute insecurity levels that have afflicted Europe in the past. Finally, we must maintain the alliance with Japan and a reasonable relation with China.

Given these policies, we will have a significant measure of arms control in the 1980s, probably focusing on the strategic nuclear forces and the intermediate-range nuclear forces that currently pose the main threat to both countries. Whether this kind of arms control leads to a 10 percent, or 20 percent, or 50 percent reduction in forces is an interesting and useful question, but it is not the primary question. The first few hundred weapons used in a war would do most of the damage. Beyond that, most weapons would not even be utilized; they would probably be destroyed or held in reserve. So even a 50 percent cut in armaments will not change the basically disastrous character of a nuclear exchange. Although we should strive toward reduction, we should not fool ourselves at to what it would accomplish.

The essential point to make about progress in arms control is that it is an attempt to manage jointly what is, after all, a joint peril. It is a halting, slow, and very frustrating attempt. Arms control agreements and negotiations have been attacked by all parts of the political spectrum because they are easy and appealing targets. Progress takes place very slowly, but it does take place. It would have been unthinkable twenty-five years ago for the Soviet Union to agree to the kind of inspection procedure they agreed to recently; it would have been equally unthinkable for the United States to agree to and to promote parity.

The heart of the matter is that the two bureaucracies, with their burden of prejudices and partial blindness, should be able to get together and make progress in managing the threat. For that reason, unilateral steps are largely irrelevant, even regardless of whether or not they might weaken us. They don't go to the heart of the matter, except insofar as they might contribute to the resumption or continuation of negotiations.

On the other hand, if we look at arms control as some sort of magic that will permit us to turn back the clock, undo what has been done, and forget about nuclear weapons, then our arms control efforts in the 1980s are doomed to failure. Furthermore, we would be risking the continued preservation of peace.

Arms control is part of a moderate and enlightened policy. It is part of the bargain, whether we like it or not, of improving our institutions so that civilization will not perish. But arms control is not a way by which, at some level of reduction, we will eliminate the essential nature of nuclear peril.

William Potter

The major impediment to meaningful arms control in the 1980s, as it has been in the past, is more political than technical in nature. It arises from a combination of misperception, domestic bureaucratic politics, and the misguided belief on the part of both U.S. and Soviet decision makers that the fundamental security dilemma plaguing both these nuclear giants can be reduced by further arming rather than by negotiated arms control.

Indeed, there is evidence that neither Washington nor Moscow today attaches much importance to arms control as a foreign policy objective. U.S. spokesmen have argued on numerous occasions that efforts to restrain the nuclear arms race are not worthwhile and may even be dangerous until the Soviet Union has convincingly renounced its expansionist tendencies.

As a consequence, the Reagan administration has made it clear that military buildup, rather than arms control, is the first priority of U.S. foreign policy. It links arms control to Soviet foreign policy restraint, yet acts as if such restraint can be elicited only by a policy of confrontation, verbal hostility, and a major military buildup. A cynic might conclude that the present administration believes that arms control is best achieved by first letting the political relations between the two superpowers deteriorate.

Political obstacles to arms control in the 1980s, however, extend well beyond the present administration's insensitivity to Soviet perceptions, a problem that is intensified by the failure of universities to adequately support Russian language and area-study training. The political problem is the growing demands placed upon a nuclear deterrence policy at a time when the credibility of our deterrent posture is increasingly, if mistakenly, subject to attack because of alleged U.S. strategic vulnerabilities and Soviet military advances. In effect, too much is being asked of our nuclear deterrent. The most straightforward way to restore credibility to our nuclear deterrent is not to develop improved warfare capabilities, as Robert Grey and others have proposed, but to adopt a nuclear declaratory policy that repudiates the use of nuclear weapons for anything other than retaliation against an adversary's first use. For this reason among others, Ambassador York's proposal on eliminating battlefield nuclear weapons from the European theater is very compelling, although he understates the verification problems, particularly those associated with the political demands of verification.

Another political or, more precisely, perceptual obstacle to arms control in the 1980s is a tendency on the part of Western analysts to overcorrect for the Mirror Image Fallacy, that is, the tendency of Western strategists to assume that their Soviet counterparts perceive arms control concepts— such as deterrence, mutual assured destruction, deterrent stability, etc.— the same way they do. In place of this fallacy, we now have an equally dangerous rule of thumb, which some have called the Reverse Mirror Image Fallacy. It is the assumption that the Soviets cannot possibly share our perceptions about strategic concepts and issues. Today, this line of reasoning seems to dictate the repudiation of every Soviet arms control proposal or gesture without consideration of its merit, on the assumption that if the Soviets proposed it, it must be incompatible with our interests. This perspective is reinforced by the tendency—particularly acute in this administration—to assume that it knows the sources of Soviet conduct and therefore need pay little attention to what the Soviets say or how they perceive U.S. behavior. To continue to act in this fashion is to guarantee a self-fulfilling prophecy, but one that does little to enhance U.S. security.

In conclusion, there are two modest things that could be done, and they merit serious attention. A number of years ago Marshall Shulman, who at the time was a top adviser to Secretary of State Cyrus Vance, complained about the lack of skilled analysts on Soviet affairs in this country. He suggested that we would be buying more in the way of security if we applied the money spent on a single strategic bomber to train several dozen young scholars in the Russian language, area studies, and arms control policy. Our universities have yet to take Shulman's advice fully to heart. Unless we can reverse the disturbing trend of cutting back instruction and student fellowship support in the Russian area, we will find ourselves in a poor position to negotiate with an adversary whom we don't understand—regardless of the military balance.

Just as it is incumbent on the university to train specialists on Soviet affairs, so it is incumbent on present Soviet analysts to remind our policymakers that while the United States and the Soviet Union are ideological adversaries and military rivals, there are, nevertheless, important similarities and possible areas of covergence. Especially today, when the superpowers are at odds over so many nuclear issues, it makes sense to explore the possibility of cooperative action in areas such as nuclear nonproliferation where United States and Soviet interests and policies have frequently converged in the past.

Specifically, it might be possible to devise both tacit and formal means of cooperation regarding the completion of the Treaty of Tlatelolco, which calls for a Latin American nuclear-free zone. The United States and the Soviet Union might also cooperate to create additional nuclear-free zones, to develop regional nuclear fuel centers, to coordinate responses to proliferation threats (perhaps modeled after joint Soviet-U.S. action taken against South Africa in 1977), to establish joint research efforts to improve safeguards of the International Atomic Energy Commission (IAEA), and to begin routine consultation on nonproliferation problem areas—perhaps in a form similar to the Standing Consultative Commission, which was established in conjunction with SALT.

Such steps, while unlikely to lead to any major breakthrough in arms control, would serve the useful purpose of reminding both sides that their interests are not always incompatible.

Part 3

Arms Control and Technology

5
Does the Technological Imperative Still Drive the Arms Race?

Marvin L. Goldberger

Nuclear Weapons

The most striking examples of the technological imperative (meaning whatever *can* be built should be built) are found in the area of nuclear weapons. As we all know, the possibility of nuclear explosions occurred to many people immediately after the discovery of nuclear fission and confirmation of the fact that several neutrons are emitted in the act of splitting the uranium nucleus. The Manhattan Project was established with the goal of building a bomb before the Germans did. It was widely believed that they had the jump on us and that we were in a race for our lives.

When the Allies began moving into Germany following the invasion of Europe, a team of scientists led by physicist Samuel Goudsmit was sent in to assess the accomplishments of the Germans. To their surprise, the group found that the Germans didn't even have a serious reactor design, much less achievement of an uncontrolled chain reaction—a bomb. The Goudsmit Report was our first indication that we were far ahead in the race. Yet apparently no one on the project suggested that since we were not going to be threatened by the Germans with nuclear weapons, perhaps we should cease developing them ourselves. Of course, the war was not over, and we still had to contend with the Japanese. So, as the war in Europe ended in May 1945, we pressed on to the first test at Alamogordo, New Mexico, in July 1945. In the movie *Day After Trinity*, Robert R. Wilson, who was at Los Alamos during the war and was intimately involved in development of the bomb, remarked that neither he nor any of his colleagues ever raised the question of whether to go ahead with the bomb. When asked about their recollections, both Hans Bethe and Robert Bacher said they felt that the investment of time, thought, and energy by the scientists was so great that they simply had to keep on going to see if they could make it work.

The question at issue is not the subsequent use of the bomb against Japan, or whether any suggestion by the scientists not to proceed would have carried any weight with the government, which it almost surely would not. But rather, we must ask why no one even considered canceling the work on the bomb. It is evident that the technical and emotional momentum involved in the Manhattan Project was simply irresistible, and it carried over after the war. When the Baruch Plan to put nuclear weapons under international control collapsed, the U.S. military establishment, aided and abetted by our duly elected representatives, enthusiastically embraced the prospect of a better and bigger bang. We frequently overlook the fact that the military is not ultimately responsible for arms acquisition. They are often faulted for overenthusiasm when they are simply doing what they perceive to be the job we have assigned to them.

Thermonuclear Weapons

The next and truly glaring example of the technological imperative is the development of thermonuclear weapons. These weapons, which utilize the fusion of hydrogen isotopes, raise the possibility of devices of unlimited explosive power. A hydrogen bomb had long been the dream of Edward Teller, even during World War II. Yet when the decision was made to pursue a vigorous development program, no realistic design was seen on the horizon. The decision to proceed anyway was made in opposition to the now famous report by the General Advisory Committee of the Atomic Energy Commission, dated October 30, 1949. In a minority opinion, which differed only insignificantly from the main text, Nobel Laureates Enrico Fermi and I. I. Rabi said: "It is clear that the use of such a [thermonuclear] weapon cannot be justified on any ethical ground which gives a human being a certain individuality and dignity, even if he happens to be a resident of an enemy country." And later, "The fact that no limit exists to the destructiveness of this weapon makes its very existence and the knowledge of its construction a danger to humanity as a whole." This strong moral injunction against proceeding with the program was buttressed by the fact that we had more than enough fission bombs to satisfy any rational military requirements and a bomber fleet to deliver them.

However, the political climate in the country was such that there was no stopping the program. At a meeting in Princeton in June 1951, Edward Teller described how to build an H-bomb in a way that Robert Oppenheimer spoke of as "technically so sweet that you could not [as had been the case in 1949] argue about that. The issues became the military, the political and the humane problems of what you were going to do about it once you had it." Again, as in the case of the fission bomb, the excitement of having cracked this technical problem proved irresistible to the military and to our national leaders. Nothing could have stopped the program at that point. The H-bomb opened a new era in warfare and raised the specter of near total destruction of life on earth.

No other technically "sweet" thing has jeopardized world security quite so profoundly. But, without any doubt, a number of evolutionary developments have fueled the arms race. What they have done to perceptions and realities of international security is a matter for discussion.

Antiballistic Missile Defense

Another example of technological imperative is ABM defense. Following the development of ICBMs and nearly coincident with their deployment, a great deal of effort went into devising a system to defend against them. (Perhaps one should raise the question of whether ICBMs themselves are an example of the technological imperative. After all, we had intercontinental strategic bombers that could do an adequate job of nuclear weapons delivery. Once again, the opportunity presented by missile technology for much more rapid, accurate, and virtually unstoppable delivery systems proved to be a major factor in the arms race.) The ABM is being singled out here because of the overwhelmingly stupid character of that system, whose only claim to existence is that it could solve the seemingly impossible problem of hitting a bullet with a bullet.

Even though it was a marvel of computers, radar, and missiles, the ABM was evidently totally ineffective at enhancing national security. Although it was mercifully laid to rest by the SALT I Treaty, its possible efficacy is again being discussed in light of alleged new technical developments—technological imperatives, if you will—that unfortunately raise the possibility of a new impetus to the ABM aspects of the arms race.

Multiple Independently Targetable
Reentry Vehicle (MIRV)

One of the most devastatingly destabilizing elements introduced into the arms race is the multiple independently targetable reentry vehicle (MIRV) (a technological imperative historically related to the ABM program). Decoys to accompany reentry vehicles make nationwide ABM defense virtually impossible. Early on, it was realized that the most effective way to prevent discriminating decoys from the real thing was to make *all* the things real. In the mid-1960s, the United States developed a scheme by which a missile lofted a "bus" from which a number of warheads could be sequentially released. If desired, each one was capable of hitting targets dispersed over hundreds of miles. This provided an immediate multiplication of the number of warheads that could be dispersed by a given number of launchers, thereby allowing significant changes in military strategy and tactics. It created the ability to overwhelm ABM systems by sheer numbers; it greatly increased the target list; and it meant that we could attack the enemy's ICBM force with a modest fraction of our own, rather than on a one-to-one missile basis.

We were prepared to propose a ban on MIRV deployment to the Soviets in 1968 at the time of the Czechoslovakian invasion. Yet in spite of the fact that there was no Soviet ABM to penetrate, and in spite of our professed rejection of a counterforce strategy, we allowed our superior technological capability to push us into MIRV deployment. Not surprisingly, in the mid-1970s, even with ABM essentially banned by SALT I, the Soviets began their own MIRV deployment. It is clear that the technological imperative again led us to lesser, rather than greater, security.

Cruise Missile

The cruise missile is also a case study of some interest. Although these missiles had been around for a long time, it wasn't until the early 1970s that people began talking about them seriously. Some arms controllers became nearly schizophrenic over their possible effects on national security and future negotiations. Evidently, the possibility of loading the torpedo tubes of attack submarines with cruise missiles poses arms control problems. On the other hand, their existence reduces the likelihood of succumbing to certain technological imperatives. For example, highly sophisticated aircraft are not needed to penetrate Soviet airspace if a cruise missile capable of delivering a nuclear weapon within ten meters of a designated target can be released fifteen hundred miles offshore; the missile is also harder to shoot down.

Although there is no supporting evidence, the B-52s will eventually stop running and will need to be replaced by some other cruise missile delivery platform. It is not clear, however, whether the replacement should be the STEALTH aircraft, or even if the STEALTH technology is particularly useful. Nevertheless, the argument is made that since a new plane is needed, we should build the very best that technology has to offer. General Lew Allen, former Air Force chief of staff, recently promised that the STEALTH bomber would have an effective lifetime of thirty years, just like the B-52. Perhaps if we could design "lack of confidence" into weapons systems, the temptation to use them would decrease as a function of time.

Directed Energy Weapons

A final example of the technological imperative concerns directed energy weapons—high-powered lasers or particle beams deployed on satellites or, as the press prefers, space-based battle stations. The idea is that such weapons could clear the skies of satellites used for reconnaissance, early attack warning, or communications and thus render the enemy blind, deaf, and vulnerable. Suitably distributed around the earth, these battle stations would also be capable of attacking targets like ships, airplanes, and even ground-based objects—given a splendidly clear day. But according to the proponents, their greatest utility is to provide a missile defense system capable of attacking ICBMs during their vulnerable launch phase and thus magically transform the current nuclear offensive stalemate with hostage civilian populations into a defense-dominated situation with a genuine warfighting potentiality.

It is indeed true that we can build high-powered lasers and put them in space. We could probably point them at targets we can track, and we could do damage to objects in space, most assuredly to satellites, although the task of attacking ICBMs is much more difficult. It is also true that (1) we have a variety of possible countermeasures to protect our systems (both satellites and ICBMs) against such systems, (2) there are simpler and cheaper ways of knocking out satellites, and (3) the laser battle stations themselves would be exceedingly vulnerable to attack. Particle beam weapons aren't worth talking about because they are patently absurd. We read in the press that the Soviets may be in a position to deploy a high-powered laser in space next year. Whether this is true or not, if we wanted to, we probably could do the same. But we must not allow a technical capability to push us into a new level of arms development, particularly one with such dubious military value. It would be a "Star Wars fantasy" that would serve no military purpose. Its very existence might be felt to threaten C³I and thus lead both sides further into a first-strike mentality.

Our technological prowess has tempted both the United States and the Soviets to develop weapons neither side wants or needs. We cannot and should not turn off science and technology. But we should, and we must, stop pretending that building anything that can be built will lead us to security.

6
The Threat of the Neo-Luddites

Donald M. Kerr

Reliance on technological superiority has been a keystone of U.S. defense posture. Today, however, several threats to science and technology in the United States may adversely affect the nation's security and prosperity.

Technological "Quick Fixes"

One of these threats comes from the friends and proponents of research and development (R&D) who have exaggerated confidence that crash programs in science and technology can rapidly solve national problems. This is the often suggested Manhattan Project or Apollo Program approach to technical problems. Not too many national problems are in fact amenable to the crash program approach. Following the first oil shock, in 1973, we attempted to solve the "energy problem" with rapid, massive federal spending. While this had some beneficial results in improvements in conventional technologies, it did little to advance the start-up date for complex, long-term energy supplies such as fusion reactors. We found that many programs in scientific research and development are responsive only to consistent efforts made over a long time.

We now are faced with a similar problem in national defense, the increasingly aggressive Soviet military buildup, which we may be trying to spend our way out of. This approach may be useful in making up deficiencies in readiness and supplies and buying off-the-shelf weaponry; it is not likely to be of much help in accelerating development of new, exotic, and very promising military technologies such as directed energy weapons and "brilliant" conventional weapons.

Scientific "breakthroughs" are in fact usually the result of steady progress in basic scientific understanding and gradual improvements in technological know-how. Technological advancement is usually evolutionary, not revolutionary. But certain features in our society incline us not to appreciate the steady, consistent effort that must be given to ensure a productive research and development program. For one thing, most Americans maintain a fundamental belief in the natural technological superiority of the United States. Further, some of us believe that it stems from a native U.S. genius occasionally watered by federal funding. Few of us understand the nature and demands of the research and development process itself.

Another impediment to stable R&D support is the difference between the time horizon of the political decision makers who provide funding and the twenty-year time scale that characterizes many major development projects. When the payoff is so many years in the future, it is sometimes difficult to maintain the interest of the political community against more transient but more publicized budget priorities.

The consequence of these problems and misunderstandings is a dangerous overdependence on technological "quick fixes" to national problems, particularly in the defense area. Reliance on the crash program approach can be used as an excuse not to invest adequately in day-to-day scientific and technological research. Our inadequacies in R&D investment are most troubling in the defense area. Every year since 1971, the Soviet Union has outspent us in dedicated military research and development, and in 1981 their spending was about twice ours. Even the Reagan defense program increases will merely prevent the United States from falling further behind. Besides direct investment in R&D, we need a continuing high level of production of graduates in science and technology fields and investment in research equipment and facilities.

Neo-Luddism

Other threats to technological development come from modern descendants of the Luddites. The original Luddites were primarily disgruntled and threatened laborers who broke the new machines of the Industrial Revolution, which they believed threatened their jobs. They were supported by some upper-class romantics who objected to the changes that industrialization was bringing to traditional society—in the form of large, smoky cities, the disappearance of the rural peasantry, and the like.

One type of modern neo-Luddite wants to return to simpler, supposedly happier times by rejecting the (usually exaggerated) consequences of technological progress. More prevalent in the 1970s than today, this attitude was reflected in such works as Robert Heilbroner's *Inquiry into the Human Prospect* (1974), which argued that in the last few years we have become apprised of these side effects of economic growth in a visible decline in the quality of the air and water, in a series of man-made disasters of ecological imbalance, in a mounting general alarm as to the environmental collapse that unrestricted growth could inflict.

The civilizational malaise, in a word, reflects the inability of a civilization directed to material improvement—higher incomes, better diets, miracles of medicine, triumphs of applied physics and chemistry—to satisfy the human spirit.[1]

This philosophy has led some people to advocate limits to growth and constraints on technology. Whatever its maligned side effects, however, technological advancement is the force behind the increasing ease and affluence of the industrialized world, and few people seem inclined to give them up. The vigorous efforts of the Third World to industrialize, in order to approach our affluence, show that most of the world will continue to aspire to technological development, whatever we do in the West. This group of neo-Luddites also fails to indicate how we would meet our national security needs without the technological superiority on which that security has long rested.

Although the rather romantic antitechnology arguments of these neo-Luddites can perhaps be set aside, another group of neo-Luddites presents a very different objection to technological advancement, one that we must take seriously. They claim that technological progress may in principle be a good thing and contributes meaningfully to socioeconomic improvement, but it also inevitably contributes to military technology. The advancement of military technology has led to deployment of more lethal and indiscriminate weaponry (especially chemical, biological, and nuclear weapons); political and military strategies appear to promise to use that weaponry in a massive and indiscriminate fashion. Although current weapons do not, as is sometimes stated, threaten to destroy life on earth, they do pose a threat to all organized societies and to Western civilization itself. In this sense, we must ask seriously if technological development may come to pose a threat that outweighs the benefits it can contribute.

Although we have tried to devise means to prevent or constrain the use of mass-destruction weapons, in fact the political, social, or intellectual capacity to prevent their use has not kept pace with technological advances. The tensions and rivalries between states have not been reduced; no world organization capable of preventing or containing war has arisen; the motives or inclinations of men have not improved enough to ensure that war will be eliminated.

We must address several questions: How can the catastrophe of a war that uses indiscriminate weapons of mass destruction be averted without sacrificing the essential freedom and security of the West? More specifically, what part does technology play in creating the problem, and what should be done about technology in possible solutions to it?

Solutions to the Threat of Modern, Technological War

There are two generic solutions to the threat posed by war in the technological age: (1) to control or eliminate the causes of war and (2) to limit the effects of war should it occur. Thus far, combinations of these two approaches, which are the staple of modern arms control efforts, have not succeeded.

The threat posed by the application of science to the art of war was recognized by the founders of modern experimental science, but they believed that the scientific enterprise also contained the solution to the problem it created. The purpose of modern natural science was to make man the master of nature so that he could escape nature's capriciousness and force it to work for man's benefit. The prosperity provided by science would give man the material means to develop his faculties to the full. Sir Francis Bacon stated that

> the true and lawful goal of the sciences is none other than this: that human life be endowed with new discoveries and power. The introduction of famous discoveries appears to hold by far the first place among human actions . . . for the benefits of discoveries carry blessings with them, and confer benefits without causing harm or sorrow to any.[2]

The universal prosperity made possible by scientific discoveries would allow man to escape the commands of scarcity and deprivation; insofar as these are the causes of evils among men, their demise would allow for injustice and enmity to cease. The resulting spread of democratic, just, free regimes would be coextensive with the advance of the benefits of science, leading the world toward a universal and peaceful state.

Because science made this future possible, the potential military applications of technology would not come to pose a threat to civilization. To quote Bacon again:

> If the debasement of arts and sciences to purposes of wickedness, luxury, and the like, be made a ground of objection to the inventions of modern science, let no one be moved thereby. For the same may be said of all earthly goods: of wit, courage, strength, beauty, wealth, light itself, and the rest. Only let the human race recover that right over nature which belongs to it by divine bequest, and let power be given it; the exercise thereof will be governed by sound reason and true religion.[3]

Another parallel effort to control the threat of unhampered military technology and eliminate war altogether appeared in the form of socialist and communist ideology. They both proposed to use science and new political institutions to eradicate the causes of hostility between men and states and to advance the world toward a universal and prosperous state. The socialists thought that they could develop a world common-wealth of socialist governments, which would be made peaceful by the elimination of capitalist and imperialist competition. On the other hand, the communists (the early Marxists) wanted a universal society from which governments themselves would fade away, in which all individuals would live together in affluent harmony. In the world envisioned by Bacon and in that dreamed of by the socialists and communists, technology would be only a boon to mankind, and in fact would be his prime benefactor.

Instead, the advancement of technology and the growing prosperity it brought about did nothing to ameliorate the hostilities between men and states. Communism, instead of fulfilling the promise of Marx, evolved into a permanent tyranny under Lenin, Stalin, and their successors. Soon it became evident that nations were destined to remain at daggers-drawn indefinitely and that progress toward democracy and universal peace was not preordained.

Today, because military technology has apparently outrun the main schemes to place it under rational or institutional control, the future and character of military technology are serious and conscious public concerns. It is from this failure and this concern that the arms control efforts of the post–World War II era have emerged.

Efforts to get military technology under control and prevent or reduce the consequences of war have followed several paths in recent years. One approach, advocated by the neo-Luddites, is to limit or control scientific and technological progress, either in directly military areas, or across the board. This was the approach taken in a series of articles in *Science* magazine on "Technology Creep and the Arms Race" in 1978. Efforts to constrain technology ignore several important facts, however. For developed nations, technology is bound up with the entire structure of their societies. Their economies and social and political institutions have developed in the context of technological progress. Their continued prosperity, world standing, and general national security depend on advancing technology. (Our reliance on military technology is obvious: The requirement of very advanced sensor and discrimination technology for early warning of attack and for remote verification of arms control agreements are two examples.) We depend on technology in more subtle ways for our security as well. The energy crisis, for example, showed that dependence on external supplies of some critical components of our economy can pose serious threats to our prosperity. If not remedied by development of domestic energy resources, we could be forced into military confrontation to guarantee external supplies.

For the developing nations, technological progress is even more important, for they see it as the key to movement toward industrialization and its benefits. We may admonish them about the undesirable consequences of development on some aspects of their way of life, but they remain persuaded that the goods of development are worth the consequences. They would probably be even more reluctant than we to forego the benefits of technological progress.

It can be argued that although technological progress is demanded and beneficial in the civilian sector, we should place constraints on military technology. Unfortunately, military and civilian technologies are symbiotic and inseparable. Military technology has long contributed to civilian uses. For example, microprocessors and cryptology, developed in military programs, have found wide applications in civilian equipment. Recently, civilian technology has come to play a larger role in military capabilities. Developments in computer technology and materials research, conducted in the private sector for commercial applications, have made major contributions to improving military systems.

So again, limits on overall technological advance are perhaps possible, but they would severely affect our prosperity, our world standing and economic competitiveness, and our overall national security. They would also affect our social structure, probably requiring a major (and undesired) alteration in our way of life. In addition, limiting technological progress would eliminate one of the key functions that scientific R&D traditionally plays, that of providing insurance against technological surprise and obsolescence.

If limits on technological progress or on military technology are undesirable, must we be burdened with whatever unhappy military applications they make possible? There is scope for prudence and political guidance in choosing the direction of military technology and in the weapon applications we choose to develop. It is in these areas of directing and applying technology, not in attempting to control the growth of knowledge, that some mitigation of military effects may be hoped for.

Other efforts to avert a disastrous war have tried to reduce the threat from weapons of mass destruction, preeminently nuclear weapons. The prime focus of post–World War II arms control, these efforts have a long history—beginning with the (perhaps apocryphal) effort of Pope Innocent to ban the use of the crossbow (but only against other Christians) in 1139. The technology of the longbow and the military application the English made of it at Crecy may be an example of the danger involved in falling behind in military technology. Perhaps the fourteenth century elite of France—knights in armor—saw the longbow as socially destabilizing. Whatever the reason, they failed—until more than sixty years later after their crushing defeat at Agincourt—to develop the technology that made knights in armor militarily extinct.

After World War I, treaties were designed to prohibit some of the causes and excesses of that war. Bans on chemical weapons (the Geneva Protocol) and an abortive ban on submarine attacks on noncombatant ships were examples of attempts to control excesses. Various efforts to control or eliminate armaments (the Versailles Treaty and the World Disarmament Conference), or to create a war-preventing League of Nations or "international police force" were examples of attempts to prevent war from happening again.

Since World War II, the control of nuclear weapons themselves, with both quantitative and qualitative restrictions, has been emphasized. If the arms race is itself a cause or contributor to war, as some people argue, successful agreements might reduce the risk of war. Some agreements also aim to establish stability, a balance that gives neither side an incentive or need to strike first in times of tension. And finally, nuclear arms limits or reductions have aimed (in U.S. eyes) at getting both sides to accept the MAD doctrine and to renounce strategic nuclear war as an instrument of policy.

Somewhat different approaches to arms control have been the 1946 Baruch Plan, which aimed to place nuclear weapons under international control, and the idea of nuclear weapon test bans, which might ultimately lead to the withering away of dependence on nuclear weapons.

At present, these negotiated approaches to arms control have not eliminated the threat or potential damage levels of war, although several arms control negotiations are now under way or in preparation. These include the START talks (where a new approach or on-site verification seems to be needed), the INF talks (to fill the gap left by strategic nuclear weapon negotiations), test ban negotiations, chemical and biological weapons control and conventional arms control negotiations (needed to cover the asymmetries between the military needs and capabilities of the nuclear powers).

What We Can Do

These main lines of arms control of recent years seem to offer little hope. While some reductions may be possible from START and INF talks, even those will be difficult because of the characteristics of the weapon systems involved. And even reduced arsenals would possess enormous destructive power. In addition to attempting to obtain whatever improvements we can through negotiated arms control agreements, there are two things we must do. In the short run, we have no recourse but to maintain the pace of technological advancement. The United States desires peace and the retention of the international status quo; consequently, maintaining our lead in weapons technology gives the best chance for continued peace. (Technical superiority is especially important in light of our inferiority in numbers of weapons and manpower.) Technological progress is also vital in other security-related areas (e.g., a secure energy supply and increased industrial productivity) if we are to avoid falling victim to outside circumstances and are to maintain our ability to stay out of conflicts as long as we wish to do so.

In the longer run, we must consciously exploit those promising developments in military technology that offer some hope for reducing the possible damage of war, should it start, while maintaining or even increasing our security. One trend in military technology is toward the ability to create more discriminating, less massive, more secure weapons. This development, made possible by progress in detection, discrimination, and guidance technologies, improvements in warhead lethality, and greater capability for complex battle management, may in time allow for the deployment of a credible military defense with less risk of resorting to nuclear weapons or other weapons of mass destruction. For example, multiple nonnuclear warheads might be deployed on our weapon systems in Europe, effectively taking over the antiarmor role that now can only be accomplished by battlefield nuclear weapons. Developments like this offer the prospect of a future battlefield where the destruction is limited in large part to combatants.

Technological advances may also permit development of viable strategic (and even tactical) defenses, perhaps for a time shifting the military advantage from the offense to the defense. We might then move from a strategy of mutual assured destruction to mutual assured survival. One significant military option would be the ability to ward off an incoming attack without the loss of territory or the destruction of population. To have the ability to choose appropriate responses to military challenges, without the fear of immediate impending destruction, would be satisfying both politically and militarily. To achieve that position, however, will take more than reaching some rough technological parity with the Soviets; it will take a courageous long-term investment—with high risk—to lay the scientific and then technological groundwork for a significant strategic defense not linked to instant escalation.

Besides being desirable as a way to move technology away from massive and indiscriminate destruction, such developments are necessary for U.S. defense policy. In an age of strategic parity and theater and conventional inferiority, we need to develop military forces that we are not self-deterred from using, as may be the case with our current battlefield nuclear weapons. Our military deterrent would thus become more credible and those nuclear weapons for which there is no alternative at present would be protected from criticism.

The choice of weapon systems characteristics can drastically alter the perception of their intent. For example, theater nuclear forces heavily weighted toward ballistic missiles might be perceived as a first-strike capability and thus destabilizing, while greater emphasis on cruise missiles would indicate a retaliatory posture.

Over the long run, emphasizing such developments might lead us out of the dangerous situation we now face, reducing the threat that military technology poses to our nation and our civilization. Such prospects need to be examined soberly in terms of our national needs and purposes, and a national strategy must be developed for investment in scientific and technological research and development that ensures vigorous support of the trends most suited to those national purposes.

Given the harsh realities of our world, the attempts to control military technology development proposed by the neo-Luddites hold not promise but danger. We must consider the opposite course—enhancing those technologies that allow us to reduce tensions, improve international stability, and reduce the threat to national survival. We can take this course unilaterally, without having to wait for the results of desultory arms control negotiations, without having to wait for the development of goodwill or other desirable but unlikely improvements in the political climate or organization of the world.

Notes

1. Robert L. Heilbroner, *Inquiry into the Human Prospect* (New York: W. W. Norton, 1974), pp. 19 and 21.

2. Sir Francis Bacon, *The New Organon and Related Writing*, Fulton H. Anderson edition (Indianapolis: Bobbs and Merrill, 1960), p. 71.

3. Ibid, p. 117.

Discussion of Part 3

Harold W. Lewis

The arms race cannot be discussed as if it were something existing in a vacuum, as if it were something that has a life of its own, as if it were removed from a world of international tension. It is a fact that the arms race, such as it is, occurs in a world that is not entirely benign and friendly. It is a fact that national defense is a reasonable activity for a nation.

Many college students may not believe the United States was ever involved in a just war, but in World War II we were truly all on the same side, and what's more we were right. Some people say there are nonviolent ways to solve international problems, but what nonviolent way would have solved that international problem then?

The point to remember is that the prevention of war is a worthy objective, and the prevention of nuclear war is an overriding objective because the ultimate horror of nuclear war must be avoided. However, it cannot be avoided by throwing away the concept of national defense or by ascribing villainy to the people who want to develop a proper national defense.

Military technology is not intrinsically evil. For example, we have decided not to pursue even the amount of antiballistic missile technology and deployment permitted by SALT I. We have done this for several reasons, but those reasons do not include the idea that the ABM is intrinsically absurd or intrinsically crazy. The fact is that ABM technology is extremely hard to carry out with its problems of penetration and decoys. In addition, mutually assured deterrence or destruction has been working; there hasn't been a nuclear war for a long time. Given that fact, a viable ABM on both sides would be destabilizing and therefore antithetical to our main objective—to avoid nuclear war. But the ABM is not absurd.

Twenty years ago when a number of us were working very hard on the reentry physics aspects of ABM systems, Charles Townes said, "You know, there is nothing more honorable than being able to defend your own home." That was the picture of ABM activity some of us held in those days when we worked on ballistic missile defense. There is a legitimate point of view that it is good to be able to defend yourself, but the technical difficulties are there, and in the larger sense of the avoidance of nuclear war, the destabilizing effect of ABMs would be a negative factor. It turns out, however, that the ABM is technically so difficult that neither the Soviets nor the United States can do it. In fact, it is hard to understand for what reasons—other than symbolic—the Soviets have built, maintained, and improved their defenses around Moscow. One can only hope that some things that would be destabilizing in this larger sense would also be so technically difficult that they won't happen.

The point is that I do not believe that technological imperatives drive the arms race as much as some other people do. In many cases over the years, people have continued to work on weapons problems, on the development of military technology, because it was interesting. In a few cases, the fact that it was interesting was responsible for the existence of a program. In many cases, relatively uninteresting military technology programs are worked on because if the political leadership and the nation's interests, as perceived by other people, require the work to be done, the work gets done. In general, the fact that a subject is technologically interesting and important affects only the people who are working on it and rarely affects the decision makers who, in this country, in the end, are at the budgetary level.

Unfortunately, there are too many cases where illiterate technological love for a program leads to its continuance long past its appointed demise. Charged particle beams are an example of that. This technology is widely peddled on the pages of *Aviation Week and Space Technology* and among people who are technologically illiterate because it has appeal: Wouldn't it be great to shoot things at long distances with the speed of light with no reloading requirements. So some ill-informed people in the establishment have been promoting this technology over the years. It is not crazy. It is not dumb. It just isn't very good and doesn't work. It has been kept going when in fact it has no military potential, no value for national defense. This is an example of something that is driven, in part, by the technological imperative.

To ask whether the University of California's management of the Los Alamos and Livermore laboratories drives the arms race suggests extraordinary arrogance. The University of California does not drive the arms race; international tensions drive the arms race. The arms race itself is not evil; the evil is the possibility of nuclear war, a dreadful thing to be avoided. It is probably the second worst threat to humanity, and we have to do something about it. Indeed, if I could be convinced that the best way to prevent nuclear war was to have an unrestrained arms race, I would favor an unrestrained arms race.

In William Manchester's book of reminiscences of the Pacific war in World War II (*Goodby Darkness: A Memoir of the Pacific War*), when he talks about the impending invasion of Japan, he says, "Thank God for the atomic bomb." Although not many people are inclined to express such gratitude, Manchester's words bring home the fact that such weapons are not themselves intrinsically evil. It is their use—or possible use— in a situation where the gains, even given the narrowest construction of the national interests, may be far less than the destruction wrought on the world. A nuclear war would not wipe out life on Earth, but a nuclear war between the major powers would unquestionably lead to the destruction of the civilizations of the two major powers. That is certainly true, and that is something to be scrupulously avoided.

Given the complexities of the arms race, international security, and the political environment, what can the university do? It can move toward a scholarly investigation of the causes of international tension; it can recognize that tension exists and that this is not a benign world where if we beat our swords into plowshares, everything will be all right. The university can work toward shaping an environment where, first of all, nuclear war can be prevented, or where, if it occurs despite our best efforts, destruction can be limited. But these things can only occur in a context in which our national defense is adequate to do what it is supposed to do.

About ten years ago, Daniel Ellsberg gave a talk at Princeton, after which someone in the audience asked him whether he believed the United States should have an army. Ellsberg said yes. He was then asked if the United States should have a good army. Again he said yes. But when he was asked if the people who work to give the military the best of equipment and the best of capability are doing a good thing, he said no. He said that the United States should have an army adequate to defend itself against the impending threats to its security, namely, the armies of Canada and Mexico—no more. This view is not shared by the majority of the American people, who, after all, decide the direction of military technology.

Although, amusingly enough, some Americans still cannot believe that Ronald Reagan was elected president of the United States, the fact is that he *was* elected—and by the American people. The people do have a role in deciding what kind of military establishment they want and for what purpose. And that purpose reflects their view of the level of hostility of the world around them.

Jack Ruina

Although we must depend on military technology, there are good reasons to fear its adverse effects. There is a strong element of truth in the argument that military research and development is often a mindless pursuit of both the technologically possible and impossible because, unlike civilian technology, it has a life of its own without the limitations or moderation imposed by market forces. This is not to say that market forces of the free economy always limit technology in the best way. Nevertheless, military technology often goes well beyond the point where it is useful to continue, as may be the case with high-energy laser technology.

Advances in military technology have clearly been an important stimulus to the arms race. The question is, how important and how significant? Defense policy, one can certainly argue, is unduly influenced by technical specialists and analysts who extend their supposed specialization well beyond what is warranted. Often a specialist in nuclear weaponry is considered a specialist in the effects of nuclear weaponry or the consequences of nuclear war. However, the pursuit of military technology is essential to allay fears about what the opponent might be doing in the technological frontier and what his capabilities might be.

It is true that we have an undue fear of technological surprise. It appears to be an exaggerated phenomenon, yet the possibility of technological surprise cannot be dismissed. To guard against it, we pursue military technology to learn as much as possible, to understand as much as possible. It is true that advances in military technology have provided cheaper alternatives as well as reduced the need for greater numbers. New military technology has made possible those few arms control agreements we have by enhancing our so-called national technical means of verification, for instance with satellite sensors.

As McGeorge Bundy has pointed out, advances in technology have added to the safety and controllability of nuclear weapons. There is no denying that. It is an exaggeration to claim that there are technological imperatives that cannot be stopped in military technology. We certainly have stopped many. We stopped the B-70's recall; we stopped the B-1 once and may even stop it again; we stopped the ABM. In other words, having stopped some military technologies, we demonstrate that the technological imperative doesn't have to be all that imperative. We can cite many examples of military technologies that are relatively benign, that have been helpful, that have made the world safer. We can also cite many technological advances that are dangerous or at least mischievous. Although we can agree that there are good and bad military technologies, we can't agree on which is which.

The pursuit of military technology by itself, however, is not the cause of the arms race. It does not in itself drive the arms race; it is only one of the components. Regardless of military advances or new systems, the arms race would continue given the political climate we have. It is certainly a dynamic factor and gives the arms race its form and direction, but it is not the only one. The current political situation, political actions, or changes in political leadership are dynamic forces affecting the arms race. Even the placement of weapons is in itself a tremendous factor in the arms race: Should we put missiles in Germany or in Europe or on submarines? This is not a new technology, but a question of location.

Thus the arms race cannot be blamed simply on military technology. The technological community tends to exaggerate the importance of technology and to understate the harm that may come from new technologies—although it is not only in military technology that you have this phenomenon. People in communication, transportation, and even medicine, presumably very benign areas, exaggerate the benefits that can accrue from those technologies and understate the troubles they may provide.

Another tendency common to every community is to think that a new technology, a technological fix, will change what is often a much more complicated situation. In almost all human endeavors, the participants frequently have a narrow-sighted view of the role of their pursuit. The real problem—the blame and responsibility—lies with the top political leadership, which determines what technologies are pursued and not pursued. It is the responsibility of this top political leadership, which presumably has a broader perspective, to consider the consequences of these choices, and also to be on guard.

Unfortunately, the top political leadership often has not done this well enough; it certainly has not sought or nourished views that are very different from those within its own establishment. It has sometimes considered other views, but it has not in any way stimulated interest for people to look at the consequences of specific technologies. This is particularly alarming in the current administration, although it has also been true of other administrations.

We can conclude that the pursuit of military technology requires more discrimination about what we pursue and don't pursue. Unilateral action by itself can go a long way in controlling particularly troublesome technologies, such as the U.S. pursuit of MIRVs, which many people saw as unnecessary and mischievous. We could also do without the Soviet pursuit of antisubmarine warfare technology, although unfortunately the Soviets do not see it that way.

Restriction of military technology by agreement is going to be difficult because it puts a strong burden on verification, and verification of technological pursuits is difficult for many reasons. For one, it is hard to separate civilian from military technology; recent advances in computer technology purely from the civilian side have had a tremendous impact on military hardware in materials and other areas as well. Even in aircraft technology, civilian technologies have been in the forefront until recently. Verification is extremely difficult, of course, in any technological pursuit, except in certain procedures that take place in the final stage of a military technology program, such as full-range testing of ICBMs or full-yield testing of larger yield weapons.

By and large, limiting technology by agreement is almost a hopeless pursuit. Unilateral restraints have much more promise and should be used more. If there were some way to get the Soviets to open up more about what they are doing, many of our fears about Soviet technological surprise and Soviet pursuits would be considerably moderated. These often unwarranted fears have provided, at least to us, a tremendous stimulus to the arms race. There has been some improvement in the last ten or fifteen years because Soviet society is more open than it was, and also because, through our technological advances, we have been able to look into what goes on in the Soviet Union to a greater extent then before.

Most important is the fact that our political leaders must get a wider set of views about the impact of our technological pursuits before they reach any final decisions. All too often the people at the top have relatively little first-hand knowledge of the technology being pursued and cannot make their own judgments independently. When they seek advice, it is essential that they listen to a broad range of views on both the impact and the promise of different technologies.

Charles Townes

Overall, technology is probably a blessing, but it is a mixed one. Technology includes good and bad aspects—some negatives and some positives, which are not easily isolated from one another.

In the context of arms control, the negatives include nuclear weapons, MIRVs, and cruise missiles. If we must live in a world of deterrence, there are some areas of submarine technology on the positive side. As a carrier of nuclear deterrence, submarines are relatively unassailable because they cannot be easily located; they can wait before responding; they give us relative stability. Another positive technological development in this context is surveillance from space, which provides information about what each side is doing and thus enhances confidence and stability.

The field of communications is a multiplex one. Some may think that because we can't have perfect communications in any case during times of stress, we shouldn't spend money on it. One example that goes contrary to that is ELF—the extra-low frequency system for communicating with submarines. ELF would allow submarines to operate from greater depths and therefore with less chance of being detected. Thus this technological development provides additional security to submarines. If all ELF systems were destroyed at the beginning of a war, their destruction would warn submarines to surface for instructions.

Another useful technological development from the point of view of stability is the increase in range of submarine missiles. A long-range weapon suitable for use on a submarine would give submarines a wider perimeter in which to operate, thus increasing submarine safety.

These pros and cons are intimately mixed. There is also an intimate mixture of military and civilian technology that is difficult to unscramble. For example, the first laser proposed, with a power of about one milliwatt (just enough to feel if put on a sensitive part of the skin), was a scientific instrument for spectroscopy. Now people fear it as some sort of master weapon. Intense and accurate beams of particles or laser light, which do have features that are very attractive to weaponeers, are nevertheless technologically very difficult and hence can be classified for the time being as imaginary weapons. But even these still imaginary weapons increase competitive tension and probably waste money.

Certain other technologies, in quite different realms, are almost universally judged as good and lead both to stability and to human happiness. In this category, one might include the more efficient production of food, the more efficient production of useful goods, and birth control technology. Many developments with obviously good uses inherently involve dangers. One probably cannot understand how to control cancer, for example, without also knowing how to produce it.

Although any society may use judgment about which technology to emphasize, it is practically impossible to halt the development of technology, even by mutual agreement. We can exercise restraint in pursuing some fields, but we cannot accept a proposal to stop thinking or eschew examination of a new technology that we know may be examined elsewhere and result in a dangerous surprise. In the submarine case, with its close interplay between offensive and defensive methods, the important technology of detection is under continual development—on one hand, to develop techniques for better detection, and on the other, *not* to be detected. This game of detection can be played secretly and hence would be a difficult one to control. Obviously we would be surprised and made very uncomfortable by a new and successful possibility of localizing submarines.

Time delay is another factor to consider in the problem of surprise. We may need to be advanced enough in technological ideas and in science to foresee the range of possible developments and counter them if necessary, even though we may choose to exercise self-restraint and not produce or emplace certain types of weapons.

In sum, while self-restraint is a possibility, the enforcement of a complete cut-off of technology is essentially impossible—and may be limiting from the point of view of benign or highly desirable human advances.

Part 4

Arms Control and
International Security:
Europe and the Soviet Union

7

The Soviet View
of the Strategic Situation

Jerry F. Hough

Nothing is more complex than the assessment of the strategic situation of a superpower in the nuclear age. It can be defined in terms of the degree of the security of the country or its ability to achieve specific interests. It can be defined in terms of the balance of nuclear weapons either at the present or after a hypothetical first strike by the adversary. It can be defined in terms of losses and gains of small pieces on the chess board. Frequently, analysts assume that the strategic situation can be calculated rather precisely and that the different variants of its definition can be aggregated into a single assessment. The shift of one small Third World country from one side to another, the acquisition of a base by one side, or even the Soviet purchase of a computer can be treated as being of great strategic importance.

Yet, in reality, the situation is far more complex. Compare, for example, the world situation today with that in the late 1950s. On the surface, enormously significant developments have occurred. Intercontinental ballistic missiles have been installed, and the Soviet Union has acquired a retaliatory capability that gives it parity with the United States. The Soviet Union has also developed a deep-water navy and has acquired new bases. The United States has lost the Vietnam War, and the Soviet-Chinese conflict has been the most dramatic event in the shattering of the world communist movement. West Germany and Japan have risen from defeat to become the two most dynamic of the industrial giants.

If, however, one looks at the U.S. press of the late 1950s, it is striking how familiar the image of the world situation is to a contemporary reader. Then, too, the United States was absorbed by its military weakness, with near hysteria produced by the Soviet Sputnik and a looming window of vulnerability—the missile gap. The Soviet-U.S. competition in the Third World was at the center of attention. Cuba was becoming a Soviet ally, ninety miles from our shore; a "national-liberation war" in Vietnam was a nagging concern; Egypt and Iraq were seen as Soviet proxies posing a major threat in the Middle East and North Africa; a large number of new post-colonial leaders (for instance, Sukarno and Nkrumah) described themselves as socialists and, although professed neutrals, generally supported Soviet foreign-policy positions. When Leonid Brezhnev became chairman of the Presidium of the Supreme Soviet in 1960, one of his first foreign travels was to black Africa, the first such visit by a Soviet leader. Perhaps not totally by coincidence, Patrice Lumumba was killed while Brezhnev was on the continent.

And, finally, the young Henry Kissinger was exploring the dilemmas of the nuclear age in his first major book. Because of the U.S. ability to retaliate with nuclear weapons against a massive Soviet land attack against Europe, there was need to reassure the Europeans—and the Soviet Union—about the credibility of our deterrence. He wrote mainly of the use of limited nuclear weapons in the defense of Europe, but he was fully aware that such a strategy might raise many fears among Europeans that their homeland might be destroyed in its defense.

There are a number of reasons for the difference between the apparently enormous changes in the world over the last quarter of a century and similarity in the U.S. perceptions in the late 1950s and the early 1980s. Basically, to a degree that is not widely appreciated, the factors that traditionally have been associated with strategic positions in the days before nuclear weapons and the existence of superpowers have often declined in importance. Nuclear weapons and the ability to deliver them mean that buffer zones and allies are not as crucial as in the past. The movement of a country from one side to the other just does not make the same difference to a superpower's fundamental security that it once did.

The other side of the coin, however, is that the causes of insecurity have multiplied. First, of course, it is difficult to shake the belief that old factors still might matter—that maybe Grenada's proximity to shipping through the Panama Canal, for example, is militarily significant—and in certain circumstances, some of them might. Given the instability and nationalism of the Third World, as well as the sheer numbers of Third World countries, it is inevitable that revolutions will be occurring continually somewhere in the world and that the various governmental and nongovernmental leaders will try to use one or the other of the superpowers for their own purposes. Consequently, the superpower will always have small gains and losses to worry about.

Second, the ideological struggle often gives rise to anxieties that are only marginally related to the strategic balance in the immediate sense, but that can be worrying in the extreme in long-term perspective. Both sides are hoping to see the world evolve in ways that correspond to its ideology. We have seen how the Soviet efforts to promote a communist world have led many Americans to fear that the Soviets will actually be successful, and the corresponding fears about the attraction of Western values obviously exist in the Soviet Union—and, to be frank, with much greater justification. Although the United States and the Soviet Union would surely be hostile rivals even if the former became communist or the latter democratic, and even though noncommunist India is much friendlier to the Soviet Union than is Communist China, it is easy to fear that an ideological tide in one direction or the other would erode the other side's strategic position or, conceivably, its foreign-policy independence.

Third, the nuclear age has produced a kind of insecurity that is unprecedented, at least for a large country and certainly for the United States. One can speak about deterrence, but absolutely nothing can prevent a country from being utterly destroyed in a nuclear attack. In a very real sense, personal survival and the country's safety ultimately depend on the rationality of the opponent's leaders. If they become crazy enough to push the nuclear button, we can do nothing but destroy them in return.

In addition, the existence of nuclear weapons introduces an element of uncertainty into all calculations of conventional warfare. If you are absolutely convinced that the adversary—rationally or irrationally—will retaliate with nuclear weapons on your cities in response to a conventional military action you initiate, then it cannot be rational for you to initiate such an action. Yet, if one is absolutely convinced that the adversary will destroy your cities if you retaliate with nuclear weapons against his conventional attack, then it almost never can be rational for you to retaliate with nuclear weapons against his conventional attack.

Since the adversary faces the same dilemmas, the question of deterrence ultimately becomes a game of bluff and double-bluff. Problems such as the credibility or noncredibility of the nuclear umbrella over Western Europe must continually be papered over with some sleight of hand that does little to relieve the basic feelings of insecurity.

These various complexities in defining the strategic situation must be kept firmly in mind as we try to assess Soviet views on the subject. Usually, we ask whether the Soviet leaders really think that they have military superiority or how they calculate the concrete strategic balance (or correlation of forces, to use the Soviet phrase that we usually quote). These are important problems, but it is even more important to ask whether the Soviet leadership has been developing an understanding of the complexities of strategic thinking in the nuclear age. This is all the more crucial because, as will be discussed in the next section, a number of traditional "givens" in the Soviet strategic situation have changed in a fundamental manner, but policy has not yet adjusted to the changes. The crucial question for the West is whether these adjustments will start to be made by the post-Brezhnev leadership.

Changing Soviet Leadership

Any analysis of Soviet leadership and elite thinking on almost any subject, particularly strategic ones, must begin with the generational factor. Since the end of the Stalin era thirty years ago, there have been strong continuities in the way that the Soviet Union has responded to foreign problems and in the way that it has pursued its military buildup, but there have been so few changes in the leadership that one cannot determine with any certainty the extent to which we have been observing a permanent Soviet (or even Russian) foreign policy posture or one that is the product of a stable group of officials in a particular historical era.

Although there was an important change when party leader Nikita Khrushchev was removed—one that resulted in the end of such rash policy initiatives as the installation of the Cuban missiles and the ultimatums over Berlin—there has been enormous continuity in the composition of the Soviet foreign-policy makers just below this level. Brezhnev himself was the Central Committee secretary for the defense industry and top coordinator for the space program from 1956 to 1960. Mikhail Suslov had been a Central Committee secretary with ideological and foreign-policy responsibilities since 1946. The head of the international department of the Central Committee, Boris Ponomarev, has occupied his post since 1955, and had held high posts in this realm since he was appointed to the Comintern in 1935. The minister of foreign affairs and the minister of foreign trade (Andrei Gromyko and Nikolai Patolichev) were appointed over twenty-five years ago, in 1957, and Gromyko was head of the U.S. desk of the foreign ministry in 1939 and ambassador to the United States in 1943. The minister of defense, Dmitrii Ustinov, was appointed a minister of the defense industry in 1941 and was one of the top three or four defense industry administrators before he became the top man in the field in the mid-1950s. The new general secretary, Yuri Andropov, became ambassador to Hungary in 1953 and was head of the socialist countries department of the Central Committee from 1957 to 1967 before becoming KGB chief in that year. (The KGB performs foreign intelligence functions corresponding to those of the CIA as well as internal security ones.) Brezhnev's chief personal assistant for foreign policy, Andrei Aleksandrov-Agentov, held this position since 1960, and, surprisingly, Andropov retained him as his foreign policy assistant for relations with the West.

Until recently, the same situation prevailed in the Ministry of Foreign Affairs, at least among the top men for formulation of policy toward the Third World. Vassiliy Kuznetsov, the man in charge of China policy in the ministry, had been first deputy minister since 1953 and chairman of the trade unions under Stalin. Africa was the responsibility of Leonid Ilichev, a chief editor of *Pravda* under Stalin and the Central Committee secretary for ideology under Khrushchev, and Southeast Asia policy was run by Nikolai Firiubin, a Moscow city party secretary in the late 1940s. Latin America was handled by Iakov Malik, the delegate to the United Nations during the Cold War, while Afghanistan and Iran were within the province of Semen Kozyrev, Vyacheslav Molotov's chief assistant for foreign policy during World War II. Only Kozyrev still has these responsibilities, but Ilichev was replaced in the African portfolio by another 70-year-old, Nikita Ryzhkov.

In the military, too, the marshals who were the great generals of World War II have passed from the scene, but in January 1983 the first deputy ministers of defense averaged sixty-six years of age and the other deputy ministers, sixty-seven. Even the commanders of the military districts are still almost all of an age to have fought in World War II, although on a low level. The war in Afghanistan may have an impact on Soviet military thinking, but if generals proverbially plan for the last war, it is a war fought thirty-five years ago that the leading generals all know.

This extraordinary longevity was made possible by the fact that nearly all of these men were part of a very special group in Soviet history that had been promoted rapidly, while still quite young, during the Great Purge of 1937–1938. They had been among the beneficiaries of Stalin's massive affirmative action program of sending young adults of worker and peasant background to college (usually engineering college) in the late 1920s and 1930s. They thus were part of Stalin's industrialization program—a program that he had justified, first of all, by the dangers of capitalist encirclement and in the cause of national defense.

In 1931, the year that Brezhnev entered college at the age of twenty-five, Stalin gave a remarkable speech to economic managers that seemed to come straight from the heart—and it certainly is still remembered by middle-aged Russians today.

> Sometimes it is asked whether the tempo [of industrial growth] can be slowed somewhat, whether the movement forward can be restrained. No, comrades, this is impossible. . . . To slow the tempo means to lag. And the laggards are beaten. The history of old Russia consisted in being beaten continually for its backwardness. The Mongol khans beat it. The Turkish beys beat it. The Swedish feudal lords beat it. The Polish-Lithuanian

nobility beat it. The Anglo-French capitalists beat it. The Japanese barons beat it. Everyone beat it because of its backwardness—its military backwardness, its cultural backwardness, its governmental backwardness, its industrial backwardness, its agricultural backwardness. . . .

We have a fatherland, and we will defend its independence. Do you want for our socialist fatherland to be beaten and for it to lose its independence? But if you do not want this, you should in the shortest time liquidate its backwardness. . . . We are lagging behind the advanced countries by 50 to 100 years. We must make up this distance in ten years. Either we do this, or they will crush us.[1]

This speech gives great insight into the thinking of several generations of Soviet leaders. The sense of inferiority and of threat surely was genuine. The revolutionary movement in Russia had been associated with a series of foreign-policy disasters as Russia began falling behind the industrializing West in the nineteenth century. The defeat at the hands of Great Britain in the Crimean War of 1855 was followed by the political agitation of the 1860s; the defeat in the Russo-Japanese War of 1904–1905 was followed by the revolution of 1905; and then the extremely poor performance in World War I was followed by the fall of the tsar and subsequently the Bolshevik revolution. The revolutionaries not only felt these national humiliations themselves, but also learned to play upon the emotions they produced and to use them in legitimating themselves and in enlisting the enthusiasm of the young men of the Brezhnev generation.

Yet, as one reflects on the Stalin speech of 1931, it is striking how a people who were beaten so often had managed to gain control over such a vast country with so many different peoples. The Bolsheviks, with their image of a strong centralized party had gained the support of Russian workers before the revolution, while the Mensheviks, the less centralized Marxist party, had won the non-Russian workers. Everyone must always have had the sense that, despite the rhetoric about a world revolution and the withering away of the state, a centralized party meant Russian control over the non-Russian borderlands. Certainly, the Bolsheviks simply took for granted, after the revolution, that they should try to reconstitute the old Russian empire and regain control over the Russian borderlands. The sense of encirclement and of military inferiority vis-à-vis the West was not accompanied by any sense of inferiority or deference to smaller nations on the periphery of Russia proper.

To a very considerable extent, Brezhnev seems to have retained many of these traditional ideas throughout his life. Certainly, while he did tolerate considerable independence in the internal evolution in Hungary and Poland, his reactions both to Dubchek in Czechoslovakia and to

Solidarity in Poland demonstrated the limits of his tolerance. His invasion of Afghanistan indicated that his determination to preserve that which he considered "his" among the border peoples extended to a country that had not been communist but only within the Soviet sphere of influence.

Similarly, so far as the West is concerned, it is unlikely that Brezhnev ever really felt in his bones that the Soviet Union had reversed its old inferiority and achieved equality, let alone superiority. From his perspective, the relevant comparison was not the military strength of the Soviet Union and the United States, but that of the Soviet Union and all its potential enemies. The NATO countries other than the United States have one and a half times the number of U.S. troops, and the CIA calculation places Soviet military spending well above that of the United States and puts total NATO spending above total Warsaw Pact spending. And such calculations do not count Japan and China, which Brezhnev never forgot.

Basically, Brezhnev never seemed to think of the Soviet Union as a country that could seriously influence the policies of the great powers. If gestures were offered or reciprocated, he could sometimes act in a conciliatory manner. In particular, he was able to overcome the old fears of Germany and to achieve a degree of reconciliation with West Germany that would have seemed almost unthinkable at the beginning of his regime. Yet, he normally seemed to expect hostility, and he woodenly responded in a gruff manner when he encountered it. His actions gave little hint of an awareness that the Western talk of a Soviet threat might reflect a genuine fear and that Soviet actions, and even manner of doing business, were contributing to these fears.

Irrationalities in Brezhnev's Foreign Policy

The greatest tragedy is that Brezhnev never really reacted to the change in the international situation that occurred during his reign. As a result, a number of basic Soviet foreign policies that were more or less rational in the first years that he was in office became increasingly less so as time went on, but the policies were not changed.

One such irrationality involves the scale of the Soviet forces on the Chinese border. At the time of a series of border conflicts with China in the late 1960s and early 1970s, the Soviet Union sharply increased the size of its army, and it put the new units in the Far East. Whatever may be said about the wisdom of this original move, the situation was transformed in the next decade. The border incidents died down even during Mao's life, and the post-Mao regime reduced its military budget. During its war with Vietnam, China demonstrated that it could barely handle the Vietnamese army and that it will be decades before China will pose any military threat at all to the Soviet Union. The Soviet leaders may want to maintain their Far Eastern army as a threat to China in case the latter is thinking of an invasion of Vietnam, but at a time of growing labor shortages and economic difficulties, large numbers of the Far Eastern troops really should be demobilized and shifted into the civilian economy.

A second irrationality is the scale of the conventional forces facing Western Europe. There was a time when it was easy for the Soviet leaders to frighten themselves with thoughts of the rebirth of German militarism or to dream that maybe the military conquest or communization of Europe would produce major economic gains. With such fears and vague hopes, a large standing army facing Western Europe was not all that unreasonable.

All of that has changed. If there ever was the slightest reason to fear West Germany, that disappeared with a decade of Soviet-German détente that survived the deterioration in Soviet-U.S. relations. The split with Communist China—and the continuing difficulties with Eastern Europe— has ended any thought that a communization of Western Europe would be an automatic benefit to the Soviet Union. Indeed, with the Soviet Union now getting advanced Western technology, which communist regimes find difficult to produce, a Soviet victory in Europe might be counterproductive. War would leave a devastated continent, unable to export to the Soviet Union. The reconstruction of Europe along communist lines would undoubtedly reduce the quality of the goods that eventually were sent to the Soviet Union.

In short, the Soviet Union has no reason to fear an attack from Western Europe and no interest in launching an invasion. It cannot even hope that its military strength will have a political impact in Europe. If one country convinces another that it will utilize superior forces, that has a political impact, as certainly was the case in Poland in 1980 and 1981. However, military forces that a country is known to be unwilling to use bring no political benefits. The Soviet Union has been militarily superior to China, Albania, and Yugoslavia, but that has not turned them into satellites. The United States has been militarily superior to Vietnam, to Iran, to Cuba, and now to Nicaragua, but that has not translated into political influence.

A third irrationality is the level of military secrecy that exists in the Soviet Union. For decades the Soviet Union was weaker than the West, and military secrecy was perhaps useful in hiding the level of Soviet weakness. With the achievement of general parity, however, the secrecy has become deeply counterproductive. The Soviet Union has only 65 percent of the GNP of the United States and only some 20 percent of that of the United States, the other NATO countries, and Japan combined, and it has no chance of outspending all of these countries in an arms race. Hence the Soviet Union has a vital interest in capping the arms race, and this can be done only if it reduces its threatening image. The military secrecy means that the Soviet Union is relying on the Pentagon and the CIA as the sole source of information about the size of its military and its military buildup. They are scarcely the most unbiased press agents, and even their estimates are open to unanswerable attack by those who want to paint an even darker picture.

The Brezhnev regime gave an occasional sign that it understood the need for change. At long last, the general secretary began to state unequivocally that he did not believe in the winnability of nuclear war, and the Soviet Union did release a little information about the weapons in the SALT categories. It made some gestures to the post-Mao Chinese regime and even announced a tiny reduction of troops in East Germany.

Nevertheless, Brezhnev either could not bring himself to believe that the situation had really changed, or else he could not bring himself to do the things that might have had a serious impact. He reacted very quickly to hostility or even slights. Thus, although he had stated that détente did not signify the end of ideological struggle, he grossly overreacted when the Carter administration took him at his word and launched its human rights campaign. Relations with Western Europe, China, and other countries, such as Japan, were conducted woodenly.

The way in which the Soviet Union handled the installation of its SS-20s in Europe is a perfect illustration of the problem. It had 650 aging missiles aimed at Europe, each with a single warhead. If it had announced that it was replacing them with 175 SS-20s, each with three warheads, and treated the reduction of 125 warheads (and a proportionately bigger reduction in megatonnage) as a "peace" gesture, it would have created relatively little stir. Instead, the Soviet Union simply began installing the new missiles without announcement. It did not promise any limitation in their number and said nothing about replacing the old SS-4s and SS-5s. As a consequence, all information about the missiles came from the U.S. government, which had no incentive to underestimate the program. The Soviet Union received precisely the kind of press in the West that it deserved.

The New Leadership

Now Brezhnev is gone. The inner core of the Politburo of his era—Andrei Kirilenko, Alexei Kosygin, Nikolai Podgorny, and Mikhail Suslov—is also gone. The question is, Will this historic change of leadership now be accompanied by a recognition of the new strategic realities?

Will it be accompanied by a more thoroughgoing appreciation of the implications of the nuclear era and of the achievement of basic military parity?

Unfortunately, these are questions that cannot yet be answered conclusively. Certainly, there are a substantial number of men in the foreign-policy establishment who have come to think about strategic matters in very different terms than was traditional in the past. One of the major consequences of the SALT process was the legitimization of civilian interest in strategic questions. Diplomats had to study U.S. disarmament proposals and help prepare the Soviet responses. Scholars had to write articles, books, and classified memoranda, analyzing U.S. strategic thought and plans. Institute memoranda to higher authorities always had to include specific recommendations for Soviet policy.

In the process, these specialists became intimately familiar with all the dilemmas of the nuclear age and with Western thinking about them. Articles raising iconoclastic points increasingly appeared in print, either plainly or in Aesopian language: that nuclear war could not be won, that China was not a threat, that Westerners might have a genuine fear of the Soviet Union, that the strategic balance is quite stable and marginal changes in weaponry on either side cannot affect it, that threat perception is a key issue and attention should be given to the reduction of such perceptions, that large submarines are not the best retaliatory weapon.

All of these positions are controversial and part of a continuing published debate in which opposing positions are also advanced.[2] Nevertheless, the Soviet civilian strategic analysts on the whole are far more dovish than their U.S. counterparts. There are many reasons for this, including a different relationship to the military and the different structure of the scholarly community. Most important, the Soviet analysts are responsible for answering the hard-line U.S. analysts, and in the process they learn and assimilate the opposing line of argument.

But all of this still leaves us with the question of the actual policy to be followed by the post-Brezhnev leadership. As has been seen, the new general secretary has been part of the foreign-policy establishment for thirty years and turned sixty-nine years of age in 1983. The minister of foreign affairs, the minister of defense, and the head of the international department of the Central Committee have been in their jobs for over a quarter of a century and range in age from seventy-four years to seventy-eight. The instinctive assumption is that such a group of leaders is not likely to bring any fresh perspectives of any type to Soviet foreign policy or to make any significant changes in it.

Two cautionary points should, however, be made about these status quo assumptions. First, the man who was selected general secretary may be a very different quality than the other leading figures in the foreign-policy establishment. Gromyko, Ustinov, and Ponomarev are long-time professionals within the foreign ministry, the defense industry, and the international department of the Central Committee respectively, but Andropov was in internal political work until the age of forty. For nearly a decade, he was an official in the Karelo-Finnish Republic, where the dominant figure was Otto Kuusinen, an old Comintern official who was to be the leading reformist theorist of the Khrushchev period. Then, from 1953 to 1967, Andropov dealt with Eastern Europe, where the crucial questions were the internal evolution of socialist systems and where he was exposed to—and learned to live with—many different definitions of what was acceptable socialism.

Perhaps most important, when Andropov was head of the socialist countries department of the Central Committee after 1957, he picked as members of his brain trust (first called a subdepartment and later renamed the "group of consultants") a number of young men who had been vocal in advocating reform in the published journals. The first head of this group was Fedor Burlatsky, probably the most outspoken advocate of de-Stalinization in Soviet journals after 1954; the second was Georgii Arbatov, a strong supporter of détente at the time. The groups included a number of other men—for example, Oleg Bogomolov, Alexander Bovin, and Georgii Shakhnazarov—who have always been public spokesmen for a more sophisticated foreign and/or domestic policy. Andropov may never have agreed with the more radical opinions of his assistants—indeed, they differed among themselves—and his own views may have changed over the last twenty years, but it is absolutely clear that he knew what kind of assistants he was selecting, for they already were quite controversial.

The second cautionary remark that needs to be made is that the domestic situation has gradually become more worrisome and that it is impinging on foreign-policy choices more strongly than in the past. The Soviet economy has long been bedeviled by a number of problems— an incentive system that discourages innovation and the economizing of labor, a policy of price subsidy that has led to severe shortages in the stores and has prevented decentralization of authority to the managerial level, and fifty years of protectionism that has left managers indifferent to quality production and consumer desires. In the past, the impact of these shortcomings was lessened by the facts that labor was cheap and that no underdeveloped economy invents much of its own technology. With the growing sophistication of the economy, however, labor is much more skilled and valuable, the consumer is much more demanding, and the country has reached the stage of development where it should begin exporting technology if it is to remain healthy.[3]

Several factors permitted Brezhnev to postpone needed reform. His years in power featured the coming of age of the large postwar baby boom, and this alleviated the necessity to economize on labor. The price of gold and petroleum—the two major Soviet export items—rose more than ten times. The huge Western loans to Eastern Europe postponed the problems that their rising oil bills to the Soviet Union created.

In the 1980s, however, these trends have all reversed. Now it will be the children of the small group of wartime babies who will be reaching eighteen years of age. The world prices of petroleum and gold have declined significantly, and hence the Soviet Union receives correspondingly less from the sale of the same quantity abroad. Even if these prices stabilize, the windfall gain from the giant increases of the 1970s will surely not be repeated. While the present financial difficulties in East Europe are likely to be temporary, the ratio between the size of new loans and of the repayment of old ones is going to be far closer to equal than it was in the 1970s. And, of course, the Soviet Union had four bad harvests in a row, and it chose to import vast quantities of grain to maintain the livestock herds, at a cost approaching thirty billion dollars in hard currency.

Thus, on a series of questions, the rather comfortable domestic situation of the early and middle 1970s has changed radically, and the Soviet leaders realize it. If one compares Brezhnev's speech to the 25th Party Congress in 1976 with that which he gave in 1981 to the 26th Congress, the difference between the optimism, the virtual cockiness of the first speech, and the worry of the second simply leaps out. Seweryn Bialer has called the 1980s "the decade of stringency," but even more it will be a decade of choice. In many respects, the choices are as momentous as those the Soviet leadership faced in 1953 when Stalin died.

The choices will not be easy, for they are all closely interrelated. Even the early stages of economic reform will require a very painful raising of key prices, notably food prices, and Soviet leaders remember well that such an action produced demonstrations in Poland. Other aspects of social policy will also have to be attacked, namely the excessive egalitarianism in wage differentials between workers and managers and the virtual guarantee that workers cannot lose their jobs. Serious economic reform will require a vigorous attack on protectionism and a greater opening of the Soviet economy and the world economy.

For these reasons, significant economic reform in the Soviet Union has foreign-policy implications. The raising of consumer prices and other changes in social policy will be politically very difficult without a challenge to the priority given to military spending. An integration of the Soviet economy into the world economy implies a prodétente foreign policy. If the integration becomes thoroughgoing, it will be difficult to maintain the existing degree of control over the flow of ideas between East and West as well.

In short, while the economic situation in the first dozen years of the Brezhnev period encouraged procrastination in the rethinking of old policies and conceptions, the present economic difficulties will have the opposite impact. Certainly, Soviet economic difficulties are not severe enough to *force* the Soviet leaders to modify their foreign policy. Soviet economic problems were more serious in 1945 and the need for Western aid much greater, but that did not prevent Stalin from adopting policies that clearly would produce a Cold War. Yet, if the policy intellectuals with whom a new leader has long worked tell him that changes in the strategic situation suggest changes in foreign policy, the fact that the latter will help to alleviate economic problems does nothing to reduce the attractiveness of their arguments.

To repeat, however, it remains to be seen whether the changes in strategic perception that are already visible among some of the policy intellectuals will spread to the leadership level as well, especially in the immediate post-Brezhnev period. The general secretary and the leaders of the foreign-policy establishment who sit on the Politburo are quite advanced in age, and they are facing a U.S. president who reinforces old Soviet images of the foreign threat and whose military buildup makes a modification in Soviet military policy psychologically difficult.

Moreover, even if the views discussed here become dominant, one should be careful to understand the nature of the argument being made. It is *not* being said that responsible Soviet scholars, let alone Soviet leaders, are advocating a pacifist position, an abandonment of the Soviet role as a great power, or a change in the assumption that great powers are inevitably competitive. Rather, the core of the argument is that the nature of the nuclear age and the basic achievement of military parity has made a number of Soviet policies counterproductive in terms of the interests of the Soviet Union as a great power and that Soviet strategic thinkers are beginning to recognize this.

Even if the changes suggested do take place, many features of the Soviet-U.S. relationship will remain unchanged. First, no one in the Soviet Union believes that the Soviet Union should accept an inferior military position. Many do publicly argue that the intention of the Carter and Reagan administrations has been to force an increase in Soviet military spending in order to put pressure on the Soviet standard of living and consequently on its political stability. The implication of this argument is clearly that the Soviet Union should not play the U.S. game. The argument that marginal changes in the nuclear balance are not significant implies that the Soviet Union has sufficiency and need not match every new U.S. rocket, while the argument that China is not a military threat implies that the Soviet Union could reduce the size of its army. But all of these points pertain to the way that the present military balance should be calculated. They do not indicate a belief that the Soviet Union should accept the status of a second-class power.

Second, there is a very widespread feeling in the Soviet foreign-policy establishment that military equality should mean political equality. So long as the United States considers it the prerogative of a great power to try to influence Third World development, for example by helping to transport Moroccan troops to Zaire, or by trying to modify the policies of the Salvadorian government, or by financing an Israeli-Egyptian reconciliation, then Soviet foreign-policy specialists will deeply resent any suggestion that the Soviet Union has no right to engage in analogous activities. The Soviet Union may moderate its support for revolutionary movements—"human rights" in a Marxist framework, if you will—but it will never forgo competition in the Third World. This is particularly true in the Middle East. Members of the foreign-policy establishment frequently assert that the Soviet Union has a special interest in countries on its border—that Cairo is closer to the Soviet Union than Managua, Nicaragua, is to the United States and that the Soviet Union has as much right to have an interest in the Middle East as the United States does in Central America.

Third, while Soviet analysts may talk of national interest, they never can avoid ideological considerations altogether, for ideology is closely associated with the legitimacy of domestic political systems. The United States gave very minimal support to the Solidarity movement in Poland, and the Soviet aid to the rebellion in El Salvador has not been much greater. Yet, the Soviet Union can no more avoid verbal support for the rebels in El Salvador than the United States could avoid verbal support for Solidarity, and the Soviet Union found it as difficult to accept U.S. support for Solidarity as the United States does to accept Soviet support for Central American rebels. Even liberal Soviet scholars still find it difficult to adjust to the idea that U.S. support for Solidarity should be treated coolly as propaganda rather than "interference in internal affairs."

Finally, regardless of what statesmen and analysts may think in the abstract, superpower rivalry has its own logic. Thus, even when an analyst thinks that an issue in Soviet-U.S. relations has little intrinsic meaning, he may feel deeply reluctant to back off from it for fear that this will be perceived as a political defeat, with subsequent costs to credibility. Thus, most U.S. analysts think that the Pershing IIs have limited military significance, but believe that they are an important test of alliance solidarity. The same type of thinking is found on the Soviet side as well.

Similarly, even when leaders might want to conduct a subtle and differentiated competition, they never can master the enormous information about the variety of countries involved in the Soviet-U.S. competition, and hence they must delegate considerable authority to lower levels. It is difficult to avoid some simple decision rule such as "do what the other side doesn't like," and it is equally difficult to prevent lower officials with old perceptions from doing so in any case. It is also difficult to prevent "client" states or potential client states from taking actions that will exacerbate East-West relations.

For all these reasons, nothing is going to occur that will change a continuation of hostility and tension in the Soviet-U.S. relationship. A recognition of this fact is also part of sophistication in thinking about the international situation. In basic terms, Soviet thinkers, even those of the older generation, have absorbed it, for their definition of détente rests on a continuing competition, even while efforts are made to find common interests, to manage crises, and to avoid war. What they have thus far failed to do is to convince the United States that the real dangers of war or the real rewards of cooperation are great enough to warrant a meaningful détente. The task for those in the United States and in the Soviet Union who do see real dangers and real rewards is to find ways to convey this to a broader population and elite who are skeptical. Soviet adjustment to the strategic realities of the 1980s would be a big step in this direction, but the problem remains a major one.

Notes

1. I. V. Stalin, *Sochineniia*, vol. 13 (Moscow: Gospolitizdat, 1951), pp. 38–39.

2. Some of the strategic debates are described in Jerry F. Hough, "Soviet Succession and Policy Choices," *Bulletin of the Atomic Scientists*, vol. 38, no. 9 (November 1982), pp. 49–54. This article was based on the author's original speech to the conference on which this book was based.

3. For a fuller discussion of the Soviet policy dilemmas, see Jerry F. Hough, "The Soviet Succession: Issues and Personalities," *Problems of Communism*, vol. 31, no. 5 (September–October 1982), pp. 21–28.

8

Current Aspects of Security and Arms Control in Europe

Jean Klein

Introduction

Most Europeans have not been enthusiastic about arms control in the past. For example, France chose to boycott the Eighteen Nations Disarmament Committee Conference in 1962 and, until the first United Nations Special Session on Disarmament (UNSSOD), practiced the empty-chair policy in Geneva, joining the Committee of Disarmament only after it was reformed and the Soviet-U.S. cochairmanship discontinued. France was also reluctant to participate in so-called MBFR (mutual balanced force reduction) negotiations, which started in Vienna in November 1973 and have not yet produced significant results in spite of concessions by both parties.

When the arms control process began, the mood in the United States was quite different. It was assumed that agreements with the Soviet Union on the limitation and/or the reduction of strategic armaments would contribute to the prevention of nuclear war and help stabilize the strategic balance. In the 1960s and 1970s, the strategic dialogue between the United States and the Soviet Union illustrated the détente relationship between the superpowers. The United States did not consider its allies' frustrations when an agreement, not necessarily palatable to Europeans, was judged necessary to cement the common interest of the nuclear protagonists. This happened during the last phase of the Nonproliferation Treaty negotiations when the Federal Republic of Germany saw its nuclear industry threatened by a new Morgenthau plan and tried with some success to guarantee the peaceful use of nuclear energy (Article 4 of the treaty). In the same way, the agreement on the prevention of nuclear war (June 1973) was seen as weakening the credibility of the strategy of flexible response.

Under these circumstances, it is understandable that arms control raised doubts among the allies and that the consultations within NATO could not dispel uncertainties about security. Although the United States anxiously sought to reassure its allies about the political and military implications of arms control agreements with the Soviet Union, Europeans feared that their nuclear guarantor might follow hazardous paths endangering their security. Also, they knew that their capacity to influence the United States was limited.

During the last few years, the picture has changed. The word "détente" is no longer used in official U.S. statements, and arms control has acquired a bad reputation. The SALT II agreements have been judged unacceptable and their ratification postponed indefinitely. The new administration admits the possibility of resuming negotiations with the Soviet Union, but with the proviso that they should aim to reduce strategic armaments, not just limit them, which alone cannot prevent a surprise attack or consolidate the deterrence relationship. Therefore, the U.S. government has rejected the postulates honored during the "era of negotiation," refusing to credit arms control, per se, with any value.

On the other hand, Europeans have discovered the virtues of arms control as a tool to reinforce their security and to reduce the threats of an unrestrained arms race. Already in 1968, the fourteen members of the integrated NATO structure decided to try negotiating with Warsaw Pact states toward an MBFR in Central Europe. Their so-called Reykjavík appeal was made to prevent the unilateral withdrawal of U.S. troops stationed in Europe. Force reductions were also conceived as a way to improve European security at a decreased level of armaments.

Today the main concern is to stabilize the East-West relationship by limiting intermediate-range nuclear forces (INF) according to the double-track decision adopted by NATO on December 12, 1979. It is understood that the United States is willing to deploy 572 Pershing II and ground-launched cruise missiles (GLCM) on the territory of five European states from 1983 on. At the same time, the United States and the Soviet Union are invited to negotiate an arms control agreement, the results of which may eventually postpone if not renounce the modernization of U.S. nuclear forces in Europe.

Thus arms control was one of two tracks foreseen by NATO in relation to the modernization process. European countries directly concerned were eager to see the negotiations start. Nevertheless, after the Soviet intervention in Afghanistan, the future of the SALT process was debatable, and the new administration publicly expressed reservations about arms control. European governments, spurred by large peace movements, exerted pressure on their U.S. partner to come out in favor of arms control; they succeeded to a degree when Andrei Gromyko and Alexander Haig announced in September 1981 that INF negotiations would begin in Geneva on November 30, 1981. These negotiations can only lead to satisfactory results if conducted in the SALT framework. So Europeans asked for a quick resumption of the strategic dialogue between the two superpowers. In their view, a negotiation restricted to INF limitations could have a decoupling effect and give the impression that the aim was to shape a "Eurostrategic" balance. They wanted to correct the imbalances that threatened to undermine the credibility of allied deterrence strategy. This aim, however, could be achieved only if all components of the global balance were taken into account. In this respect, the coupling of the INF negotiations with the SALT or START talks was considered a condition sine qua non.

France, however, retreated from a purely critical attitude toward arms control and promoted international security at both global and regional levels. In 1978, using the opportunity of the UNSSOD, France made various proposals aimed to draw the disarmament talks from the deadlock in which they were trapped. At an institutional level, France suggested reform of the negotiating and deliberating bodies, emphasizing the need to restore the former role of the United Nations in disarmament matters.

Satisfied by the creation of the new disarmament committee, France broke with its empty-chair policy in 1979. In Europe, France suggested the convening of a disarmament conference with the participation of the thirty-five signatories of the Helsinki Final Act. This conference would approach the problem through confidence-building measures before moving toward reduction of conventional weapons in a geographic area stretching from the Atlantic to the Urals. The European partners approved this scheme, and it became a common proposal of all the NATO countries, being widely discussed in Madrid at the follow-up conference of the Committee on Security and Cooperation in Europe (1980–1981). More recently, President François Mitterrand supported the double-track decision of NATO, although France was not directly concerned.

To explain this shift, we examine the way Europeans perceive their security in the new international context, the various options open to Europeans in reinforcing their security, and the role of public opinion in the peace movement.

The Weaknesses of the Western Security System

Since the conclusion of the Washington Treaty of April 4, 1949, the security of West European countries has rested on alliance with the United States. As some U.S. analysts have pointed out, the U.S. involvement in keeping the balance in Europe is one of the main achievements of security arrangements since World War II. Thanks to this firm commitment, peace has been preserved on the European continent during the last three decades.

But uncertainties that bedeviled intra-European relations between World Wars I and II remind us that a lasting security assumes that powerful states will behave in a responsible way and not shift the burden onto weaker states. Thus Europeans would view a U.S. disengagement as a radical change in their security system, one that might seal the decline of U.S. influence in Europe. This prospect is grim enough to justify the concerns raised by "revisionist" proposals[1] and by a revival of the debate about U.S. troops abroad. Some congressmen are again suggesting that troops could be withdrawn to punish those irresponsible allies who are more prone to play détente games with the East than to reinforce their defense capacities. There is some comfort, however, in the fact that the present U.S. administration is well aware of the political and military implications of a "no-first-use" pledge or agreement and recognizes that the presence of U.S. troops on European soil serves U.S. national interests as well as those of the allies. Nevertheless, the trend toward a functional disengagement will likely continue, and the alliance will soon have to confront this possibility.

Within the alliance, the main guarantee of security comes from U.S. retention of nuclear weapons. Other NATO members contribute to the common security with conventional military means; only France and the United Kingdom possess nuclear deterrents. Great Britain moved to nuclear weapons immediately after World War II, achieving significant results in the 1950s on its own. Later it benefited from technical assistance from the United States and, after the Bahamas agreements (1962), became dependent on the United States for the modernization of its "independent nuclear deterrent."

France followed another path. When General de Gaulle decided to develop a French nuclear deterrent and brought to fruition the policy of the Fourth Republic, he was sharply criticized by the U.S. administration, including Defense Secretary Robert McNamara, who staunchly opposed "independent national deterrents." Most French political parties also had reservations about the Gaullist nuclear policy but were unable to prevent the completion of the "strategic nuclear force" (*force nucléaire stratégique* or FNS). By the close of the 1960s, France had demonstrated its capacity in the nuclear field, and as the first elements of the national deterrent became operative, many people changed their minds, accepting the *fait accompli.*

In the transatlantic framework, the controversy dimmed, and in the 1970s NATO recognized the contribution of the two European nuclear powers to the "overall strengthening of the deterrence of the alliance" (Declaration on Atlantic Relations, approved in Ottawa, June 19, 1974, and signed in Brussels, June 26, 1974). In France, the main political parties abandoned their former prejudices against nuclear deterrence and, at the legislative elections in March 1978, reached a consensus in this respect. Nevertheless, debates on the European defense effort continue, and at regular intervals doubts are expressed in the United States about the presence of U.S. troops in Europe.

It should be remembered that the Atlantic alliance is not classic coalition diplomacy, in which collective security rests on the combined efforts of all member-states. As Kenneth Waltz rightly points out: "In fact if not in form, NATO consists of guarantees given by the United States to its European allies and to Canada. The United States, with a preponderance of nuclear weapons and as many men in uniform as the West European states combined, may be able to protect them; they cannot protect her."[2]

As nuclear weapons are the main tool of the security guarantee given to the European allies, and as most European allies are not willing to go nuclear or have been prevented from doing so, an enduring U.S. involvement in Europe is the only way to keep the balance that maintains peace on our continent. Any proposal to defend Europe with conventional means or to transfer to Europeans the responsibility of their own security has no chance of being accepted.[3] Even in the NATO framework, however, there are growing doubts of the credibility of the U.S. guarantee; also, three recent situations have emphasized the weaknesses of the Western security system:

1. When the strategy of flexible response was substituted for the strategy of massive retaliation, Europeans expressed discontent, but only General de Gaulle foresaw the consequences of this shift in developing the basis of an independent military policy. Although the NATO partners disapproved of his move at first, they eventually accepted the French stance. In the meantime, they too became suspicious about the deterrence that is supposed to guarantee their security.

The question of what would happen if deterrence fails and war breaks out is crucial for those countries located on the line between the two worlds. Germany, which is especially vulnerable, would be the main battlefield in a military confrontation on the continent. Debate on the credibility of the strategy of flexible response cuts across all political parties, including the CDU-CSU. An analysis of the dilemmas of NATO strategy published in the early 1970s by the Max Planck Institute of Starnberg underscored the fallacies of a rational defense of the central theater.[4] But the political and military establishments rebutted the authors' arguments, maintaining that there was no real alternative to the traditional way to guarantee the security of the Westen world.

One member of the Max Planck Institute, Horst Afheldt, later suggested a restructuring of the NATO defense apparatus.[5] He conceived a model to decrease the risks of a nuclear preemptive strike and make feasible a defense of the central area with modern conventional means used in a guerrilla mode (the so-called techno-guerrilla). Despite reservations on both the feasibility of such a defense and the linkage between this area defense (*défense opérationnelle du territoire*) and the nuclear guarantee that is considered an essential part of the whole system, these ideas have gained considerable attention.

The fact is that the perception of a shift in the regional balance, the unrelenting pace of the arms race, the qualitative improvements in the armory, allowing a counterforce use of nuclear weapons, the assumed reluctance of the United States to use nuclear weapons for the sake of distant allies, and the will to put the escalation process under tight control are a few of the factors that explain the new mood in Europe, especially in Germany. There is a greater awareness of the risks of decoupling the European theater from the U.S. nuclear guarantee. There is some sense that refining the counterforce strategy would make a war more probable. People living in Central European countries fear that the use of tactical nuclear weapons in a war would cause unacceptable destruction. The greater likelihood of a war coupled with the improvement of the means to confine it outside the sanctuaries of the nuclear powers induce more and more people to attach a stigma to the NATO doctrine as a self-deterrent, or, worse, as a suicidal defense. In short, what James Schlesinger once defined as "intrawar deterrence" is flatly rejected by the people who would suffer the consequences of such a military posture.

2. Since the beginning of SALT, Europeans have felt that bilateral arms control might endanger the Atlantic alliance and undermine the credibility of the U.S. guarantee. To dispel these fears, the United States was anxious to keep its allies informed about what was happening in negotiations with the Soviet Union. From 1969 to 1972, during the first phase of the talks, the allies were regularly briefed at NATO headquarters and were satisfied with how Americans were handling issues. Actually, the SALT I agreements did not challenge the main security interests of the Western world. The forward-based systems, which were directly assigned to the defense of Europe and were supposed to compensate for the Soviet intermediate-range nuclear weapons, were not included in these negotiations, despite Soviet requests for their limitation, because they were considered strategic weapons and could hit Soviet territory. On the other hand, limitation of the deployment of ABMs could only be welcomed by medium nuclear powers like France, as such limitation would make it easier to penetrate the defenses of the potential adversary. Nevertheless, worries were expressed during SALT II, as the arms race

went on unabated and modernization of Soviet intermediate nuclear weapons threatened the regional balance in Europe.

In his Alastair Buchan memorial lecture (October 28, 1977), Chancellor Helmut Schmidt underlined the new problems stemming from codification of the strategic nuclear balance. In his view, "SALT neutralizes the strategic nuclear capabilities of the United States and the Soviet Union. In Europe this magnifies the significance of the disparities between East and West in nuclear tactical and conventional weapons."[6]

So it was essential to ensure that negotiations on the limitation and reduction of nuclear strategic weapons did not neglect the components of NATO's deterrence strategy. According to Schmidt, arms limitations confined to the two superpowers would inevitably impair the security of the West European members of the alliance vis-à-vis Soviet military superiority in Europe if "we do not succeed in removing the disparities of military power in Europe parallel to the SALT negotiations."[7] This being the concern of the Germans, two solutions could be imagined: (1) a limitation of intermediate-range nuclear weapons in the framework of SALT, or (2) the modernization of the Western nuclear arsenal.

During the negotiations, it was apparent that a satisfactory negotiated solution would not be obtained. The Europeans felt that in U.S. bargaining with the Soviets, the Americans were more interested in reaching equivalent ceilings for central strategic systems than in correcting regional imbalances in Europe. Europeans could not welcome the stipulations of the protocol to the SALT II treaty because constraints were on arms systems, GLCM, which might improve the Western military posture and appeared as the blueprint for future limitations of the "gray area" weapons. Finally, it seemed that the United States had lost some bargaining power, agreeing not to impose limitations on Soviet Euro-missiles in order to extract some concessions from the USSR at the strategic level.[8] This looked like a superpower bilateralism careless of the security interests of the European allies.

3. Contradictory statements made in October and November of 1981 by Mr. Weinberger, Mr. Haig, and President Reagan about how a war could be conducted in Europe have confused the allies and fueled the peace movement. Usually the hypothesis of a limited war in Europe is not discussed publicly; plain common sense recommends discretion. Although it was reaffirmed that the fate of the United States was closely tied to its European allies and that interallied solidarity remained intact, the negative impact produced by these wranglings could not be mended entirely. The growing doubts expressed today in Germany on the strategy of flexible response stem to some extent from this imprudent exposure of the intricacies of the Western military posture.

If fact, European allies who depend on the U.S. nuclear guarantee are confronted by two intriguing developments. On the one hand, they perceive that an armed conflict in Europe would not necessarily escalate to a strategic exchange and that the interest of the guarantor is to maintain the hostilities in a clearly circumscribed area. As Mr. Schlesinger said, the military response should allow, at any stage of the conflict, a political solution of the differences. On the other hand, the United States seems to be considering the deployment of defensive weapons to win a battle on the central front. For example, the decision to produce and to stock enhanced radiation weapons on U.S. territory could be construed as the first step toward their deployment in Europe. Germany, however, has voiced its concern about the meaning of such a move and expressed clear opposition to defense with tactical nuclear weapons. In any event, uncertainties in this area preclude common understanding within the Atlantic alliance and fail to reinforce the spirit of defense in those countries likely to be victims of a "limited nuclear war."

The Security Options of the Europeans

Considering the erosion of the U.S. guarantee, some European experts came up with formulas that might compensate for the shift of the military balance in favor of the Eastern side. This thinking flourished at the time SALT negotiations were ending and concerns about Soviet superiority at the Eurostrategic level were at their highest. In France, the idea of a reinforcement of the European defense was quite popular in some circles. An essay published in June 1979, after the European parliamentary assembly elections, underlined the European dimension of defense.[9] The authors—two of them were French officers—reiterated the idea of French-British nuclear cooperation, which was supposed to lead to building a European pillar of the alliance. This scheme, supposedly compatible with the global strategy of the main nuclear guarantor, would fit into the traditional philosophy of the alliance.

The late Alexandre Sanguinetti and General Georges Buis, both Gaullists, in an interview for *Le Nouvel Observateur* (August 20, 1979), explained that a European defense was not conceivable within the Atlantic framework and that nuclear cooperation with Great Britain was doomed to failure. Attempts made in the past, when M. Debré was Minister of Defense, had not been successful, and it was unlikely that such a venture would succeed in the future. The only way to solve the problem was to turn to the Federal Republic of Germany with a proposal to share the French nuclear deterrent. This proposal raised such controversy that later General Buis explained that the aim of his interview with the leftist weekly had been to present the difficulty, if not the impossibility, of a European defense. The ambiguities of this proposal, however, and the condition of its implementation—i.e., the withdrawal of Germany from NATO—were insurmountable obstacles.

Thus there was little surprise on September 4, 1979, when Hans Apel, in presenting the German White Paper on defense, said that any participation of the country in building or deploying nuclear weapons was excluded, even in the form of the financing of a French-German project. Also, then-President Giscard d'Estaing, in a television interview September 17, 1979, flatly said that France could not favor the building of nuclear weapons in Germany, that such a policy would be "contrary to the interests of France, of Germany, of Europe and of détente."

Later, two pamphlets appeared in a collection of monographs published under the auspices of the semiofficial Foundation for the Study of National Defense. One made a case for the creation of a European defense community in the framework of the European Economic Community.[10] The other analyzed the reality of a divided Europe unable to build up an autonomous defense community.[11] These conflicting views reflect the confusion that prevails in the approaches to these problems. In spite of recurring allusions to the European dimension of the security of France, this issue is no longer considered solvable outside the framework of the Atlantic alliance.

France's military policy since General de Gaulle withdrew French forces from the integrated NATO structure and put the emphasis on autonomy has been: If France has to wage a war, it should be "its own war." In the view of General de Gaulle, however, independence does not contradict the obligations of the alliance. France would still act as a trustworthy ally in case of aggression against any NATO member. This intention was confirmed by the Ailleret-Lemnitzer agreements in 1967, and although some analysts consider that in case of an attack French forces would be doomed, nobody doubts the will of France to defend Western Europe and, if possible, to use its conventional means to repel the aggressor.

Nevertheless, the main component of the French military apparatus is the nuclear deterrent, and in this respect the new government has given priority to the modernization of the nuclear forces. President Mitterrand announced in fall 1981 that France would acquire a seventh nuclear submarine equipped with ballistic missiles and that all nuclear options would be kept open. France allots a significant part (4 percent) of its GNP to military spending, and the increase in real terms of the budget is higher than the percentage recommended by NATO. In spite of the communists in the French government, the United States considers France a trusted ally today; France is scarcely affected by the swarm of peace movements in Europe.

This does not mean that the French concept of nuclear deterrence has changed or that we are witnessing a slow reintegration into NATO. The president and the prime minister have clearly discarded this possibility, and to some extent, M. Mitterrand's statements on defense sound more Gaullist than his predecessor's. Along the same line, the concern for European defense is not in contradiction with keeping an independent nuclear deterrent. The 1972 White Paper on defense stated that deterrence for the defense of the vital interests of France served indirectly the security of its neighbors. Actually, this concept of vital interests is ambiguous; who can foresee the circumstances in which the French government would use its nuclear weapons in case of a military confrontation in Europe? French interests might be endangered if hostile troops moved toward the approaches of the French borders. The fact that a nuclear response is not excluded before the attacking troops cross the Rhine introduces uncertainty into the potential adversary's calculations and may keep him from resorting to force. In this respect, the existence of a French nuclear deterrent contributes to the reinforcement of military stability in Europe. This point was underlined by French Defense Minister Charles Hernu in a speech before the Western European Union Assembly on November 30, 1982.

A new element in French policy is its firm support of the NATO double-track decision of December 12, 1979. M. Giscard d'Estaing considered that a decision to improve the strategy of flexible response did not concern France directly and thus that it would be misleading for France to approve a modernization with which it could not be associated. Besides, the fourteen NATO countries had proposed to negotiate on the limitation of nuclear weapons in the framework of SALT, and there were good reasons to fear that the French nuclear deterrent would be included in this process. Because in the past the Soviet Union had looked on French and British forces as forward-based systems, their fate would inevitably be discussed during the negotiations. Nevertheless, M. Giscard d'Estaing, aware of the need for NATO to keep the balance, did not oppose measures to improve the military posture of the West.

M. Mitterrand was more explicit, and during the first visit of Chancellor Schmidt to Paris in May 1981 publicly endorsed the double-track decision. Later, in an interview for the German magazine *Der Stern*, Mitterrand explained that the modernization of Western nuclear forces should precede the negotiations, considering the imbalances at the regional level. But in a press conference September 24, 1981, and in a radio and television interview December 9, 1981, the president expressed more balanced views about the military trend, emphasizing the necessity to negotiate the reduction of such destabilizing weapons as Pershing II and SS-20.

Whatever the reasons behind this shift, and the wisdom of a move that brings France closer to the NATO integrated structure and casts doubts on the coherence of French nuclear strategy, it is clear that the new government is more concerned with the regional balance in Europe than was the case in the past.

Some observers are critical of a government that appears as a counselor but has no responsibility in the implementation of what it recommends. Others suggest that France's insistence on the deployment of nuclear forces on the territory of Germany is motivated less by the desire to keep the balance in Europe than by the selfish desire for the Pershing II to reduce France's exposure to the Eastern threat and increase Germany's dependence on the United States, thus preventing Germany from slipping to the East.

The idea of a European defense outside the NATO framework has never been fashionable in Germany. Nevertheless, at the end of the Fourth Republic, attempts were made to gain French-German agreements in the nuclear field and to lay the basis of a common defense.[12] These ventures ended when de Gaulle came back into power, and since then French-German nuclear cooperation has been out of the question. In 1976, Chief of Staff General Guy Mery suggested an extended nuclear guarantee (*sanctuarisation élargie*) in a speech at the Institut des Hautes Etudes de Défense Nationale; the suggestion was quickly silenced. Three years before, Foreign Minister Michel Jobert had raised the question of a European defense before the assembly of the West European Union, proposing that this body serve as a laboratory for the development of new ideas. But the Germans and British were hostile. With the development of the *Ostpolitik*, German leaders are becoming even more reluctant.

Seeing its security in the framework of NATO, West Germany has always been defiant toward anything that would undermine the alliance and force the Germans to choose between the United States, with its firm guarantee, and the Europeans, who lack the same military means. Germany's main concern was to keep the balance in Europe and to preserve the basis of the strategy of flexible response. Thus they often worried about the imbalances in the intermediate-range nuclear forces, voicing this concern at the beginning of the SALT process when they asked for limitation of Soviet intermediate-range missiles, a direct threat to their security. But the Soviet insistence to include forward-based systems in the negotiations was not acceptable to the allies, and the solution was postponed. As noted above, the issue was raised again during SALT II negotiations, with Chancellor Schmidt again at the forefront. The deployment of the SS-20 had created anxiety in Germany, and when Brezhnev visited Bonn in May 1978, Schmidt drew his attention to the seriousness of the problem. This concern is reflected in the Common Communiqué, which states that the two parties should not seek superiority in any area. Ultimately, the fourteen NATO members decided to modernize U.S. theater nuclear weapons if the two superpowers could not negotiate a satisfactory agreement.

As usual, the modernization was explained as a move to maintain the credibility of the flexible response strategy, not to establish a Eurostrategic balance that might be interpreted as a sign of decoupling. In addition, deployment of land-based missiles would show U.S. involvement in the security of Europe. The Soviet Union affirmed that if nuclear weapons were used against targets on its territory, a global exchange would begin and a response against the United States would be justified even if the weapons had been shot from the territory of the European states. The deployment of land-based missiles thus had the virtue of coupling the fate of Europe to that of the United States and reinforcing the solidarity of the alliance. At the same time, however, it introduced instability in the strategic balance and increased the risks of a preemptive strike during a crisis.

Public Opinion and Arms Control

The double-track decision adopted by NATO in December 1979 had little opposition in the countries directly concerned. This quiet acceptance of a hypothetical deployment of intermediate-range nuclear weapons was possible because the priority was on arms control and this decision to reinforce the Western defense potential would supposedly induce the Soviet Union to agree to limit and reduce its theater nuclear forces.

This aim was clearly stated in the resolution adopted by the Social Democratic Party on December 7, 1979. Later, the collapse of the SALT process and the election of Mr. Reagan contributed to a feeling that arms control was dead, that the nuclear arms race in Europe would go on unabated, and that the risks of a devastating confrontation in Central Europe would grow. These fears, fueled by political propaganda, were behind the huge street demonstrations in 1981. By fall, most governments had recognized the legitimacy of concerns expressed by the "future victims of a limited nuclear war." President Reagan, in a speech delivered on November 18, 1981, reassured Europeans about U.S. objectives in NATO and in arms control.

Peace movements quickly gained a wide constituency in the Nordic countries, the Netherlands, and West Germany. Although less impressive in Italy, a strong antinuclear trend is evident, with some people objecting to the deployment of cruise missiles in Sicily. In Great Britain, the tradition of peace marches of the 1960s continues, but with a new ingredient, an appeal for a European nuclear-free zone.

The peace movement in France is limited; the French seem less exposed to the pacifist virus. After the spring 1981 electoral success of the Left, the Communist party collected signatures for banning the neutron bomb and organized a rally in Paris on October 25, 1981. Attendance was smaller than the crowds that had gathered in Bonn and Amsterdam a few weeks before. Its limited success can be explained in part by the fact that the Communist party and the "Peace Movement," a branch of the World Peace Council, played major roles in the demonstration.

Peace marchers are often denounced as pacifists or neutralists, terms most of them object to. As peace movements occur mainly in the Western world and are either nonexistent or under stringent control in Eastern countries, some people conclude that they are inspired by communists and that demonstrations against nuclear weapons in Europe are masterminded by the Soviets to stop implementation of new U.S. missiles on the continent. In this context, the peace marchers are supposed to play the role of the "useful idiot," to quote Lenin, and serve objectively the Soviet expansionist policy. Others who believe the pacifists are motivated by the crisis of Western security[13] see the peace movement as a genuine expression of concern on the part of many Europeans.

As for Germany, the uncertainty of the credibility of the U.S. guarantee and the way Europe would be defended if deterrence fails are plausible reasons for its concern. It is too simplistic to describe as pacifist or neutralist a behavior that can be easily explained by valid and sophisticated reasons.[14]

Public opinion polls show the percentage of true pacifists in Germany to be no more than 8 percent; about 70 percent of the Germans consider that their security problems cannot be solved outside the NATO framework. Moreover, the dominant mood of the country is anticommunist; a majority of Germans contend that in case of an Eastern invasion they would resist with any means. These factors have to be taken into account to appreciate the motivation behind the German peace movement.

The only question that warrants discussion is the national identity of the Germans and a solution to that problem. The prospect of a reunited Germany through the neutralization of the two existing German states is causing growing concern in France. At the beginning of 1982, Jean Poperen, a leading Socialist personality, expressed such concern in *Le Nouvel Observateur* (January 9, 1982). M. Mitterrand and Mr. Schmidt discussed the issue during their meeting in Paris at the end of February 1982. Writing in the January 1982 issue of *Défense Nationale*, Professor François-Georges Dreyfus, an expert on German history, emphasized the national feelings of the Germans and the continuity of the West German policy about unification of the nation. Also, one cannot ignore the fact that the German peace movement is not immune to nationalistic overtones.

Since the beginning of the 1970s, the German Left has been reconsidering the national dimensions of its actions. Rudi Dutschke was one of the first leading personalities to focus attention on this point. In 1978, a collection of essays on the Left and the German question was published in Germany.[15] The ideas expressed in this book inspired the Alternative Movement program in West Berlin in spring 1981, a program that links a search for peace with the reunification of Germany.

At the same time, a prominent German writer, Martin Walser, announced that he could not recognize either East or West Germany, but wanted to keep open the "wound which is called Germany." It is not surprising that the same Martin Walser was one of the signatories of East German scientist Mr. Havemann's open letter to Brezhnev (November 1981) in which he argued for the withdrawal of the two German states from their respective alliances and suggested that they could solve their problems alone.

Finally, Chancellor Schmidt obviously uses every opportunity to remind us that the unity of the German nation is part of the constitution (*Grundgesetz*), and that he would be disloyal to his oath if he neglected this fact.

In these circumstances, it is unlikely that the German question will vanish; we can safely assume that it will be raised during the debates on security and arms control. Nevertheless, to solve the German question by neutralizing the two German states is not plausible considering the Soviet Union's reluctance to start a process that could destabilize the whole socialist community in Eastern Europe. There are always speculations about Stalin's note of March 1952 proposing the reunification of Germany in exchange for its neutralization. Today most historians consider it an ambiguous move, and Ambassador Wilhelm Grewe, a close assistant to Chancellor Konrad Adenauer, has expressed doubts about the seriousness of Stalin's proposal.[16]

Contradictions may occur in the future between a policy that claims to be tied to the West but pursues the development of cooperative ventures with Eastern countries at the same time. This combination of openness to the East and close cooperation with the Western allies could be exposed to difficulties, considering the divergent views of the United States and the European Economic Community. And as West Germany has chosen to solve its national problem by trying to keep the positive results of the détente process and by developing cooperation with the East, it might be vulnerable to Soviet pressures and be induced to argue in the Atlantic councils for a policy that could reconcile its national interests and Soviet requests.

German leaders recall that the philosophy of the Harmel Report adopted in December 1967 is still valid and that the double-track of détente and defense is the only way to solve security issues. This way, which is not a neutralist one, is proposed by the most imaginative and lucid German politicans, and analysts like Egon Bahr, Gunter Gaus, and Peter Bender. Bahr was clear about the necessity of keeping the alliance in his book *Was wirden aus den Deutschen?*[17] and in his speech at Rastatt when he received the Gustav Heinemann citizen prize (May 23, 1982). Gaus, in pleading for an active German policy, does not neglect the need for stability.[18]

On the other hand, the prospect of a Germany solving its problems without having to care about its neighbors' interests is rejected by the majority of responsible leaders and analysts, as evidenced by a sharp rebuttal to Havemann's solution by Professor Hans Ulrich Wehler and a comment by Heinrich August Winkler.[19]

The latest polls show that a majority of West Germans (62 percent) want a reunification of Germany, but only 13 percent consider this prospect realistic. The only way to satisfy the aspirations of the Germans is to contribute in a step-by-step approach to the decrease of the confrontation on our continent, and to envision the rapprochement of the two German states in a Europe that will have overcome its division into two antagonistic systems. This prospect, suggested by General de Gaulle in his press conference of February 4, 1965, is referred to by Peter Bender in his book *Das Ende des ideologischen Zeitalters: Die Europäisierung Europas*, in which he tries to solve his nation's dilemmas in a pan-European framework.[20]

Conclusion

Let us look at the converging interests of the two main continental powers, interests that exist in spite of their different situations and the specificity of their security policies.

They are anxious to keep the military balance in Europe. France is modernizing its nuclear deterrent, and Germany is improving the conventional component of the alliance. Both approve of the process of negotiation and hope that ongoing and future talks will eventually lead to a limitation if not a reduction of armed forces. They greeted the start of the INF negotiations in Geneva and the announcement of the revival of strategic arms reduction talks.

Nevertheless, France and Germany differ in their appreciation of the conference on MBFR. Germany instigated this venture, but France refused to be involved. They agree, however, on the idea of a conference on disarmament in Europe as a follow-up to the CSCE. Finally, both are convinced that there is no alternative to U.S. involvement in Europe to maintain security.

Thus it would be a pity if the present crisis in transatlantic relations results in the crumbling of security arrangements made during the Cold War, which have persisted into the era of détente because they were the basis of any improvement in relations with the East. We can hope that Europeans and Americans will overcome their current difficulties and avoid the major inconveniences of a disengagement policy that might be the beginning of a major shift in the global balance of power.

Recent trends in U.S. foreign policy, notwithstanding the withdrawal of Secretary of State Haig, seem to indicate that European security interests are understood to some extent in Washington and that the crisis will be resolved. If the price to pay is serious negotiations with the Soviet Union to stabilize the nuclear balance, it would not be too high, considering the necessity for the two superpowers to keep in constant touch with each other to counter the threats of the nuclear age.

In more general terms, however, permanent negotiations with one's adversary is not a weakness. A great statesman, Cardinal de Richelieu, did not neglect this way to promote his aims. The results he achieved in shaping the security system of Europe after the Thirty Years War were not negligible. His example should be followed by our contemporaries in the international arena.

Notes

1. See McGeorge Bundy, George F. Kennan, Robert S. McNamara, and Gerard Smith, "Nuclear Weapons and the Atlantic Alliance," *Foreign Affairs*, vol. 60, no. 4 (Spring 1982), pp. 753–768.

2. Kenneth Waltz, *Theory of International Relations* (Reading, Mass.: Addison-Wesley Publishing Co., 1979), p. 169.

3. See, for example, Samuel T. Cohen, "Armes à radiations reforcées, euro-missiles, et destin de l'OTAN," and Pierre Marie Gallois, "Irréparables, les fauts transatlantiques," in *Politique Internationale*, no. 15, Spring 1982.

4. Carl Friedrich von Weiszäcker, ed., *Kriegsfolgen und Kriegsverhütung* (Munich: C. Hanser, 1971).

5. Horst Afheldt, *Verteidigung und Frieden: Politik mit militaerischen Mitteln* (Munich: C. Hanser, 1976).

6. In Wolfram Hanrieder, ed., *Helmut Schmidt: Perspectives on Politics* (Boulder, Colo.: Westview Press, 1982), p. 26.

7. Ibid.

8. Interview with Paul Warnke, *Arms Control Today*, vol 9, no. 5 (May 1979), pp. 3–8.

9. René Cagnat, Guy Doly, and Pascal Fontaine, *Euroshima, Construire de l'Europe de la défense* (Paris: Editions Média, 1979).

10. Jean-Paul Pigasse, *Le Deuxième Pilier: Données et Réflexions sur la sécurité Européenes* (Paris: Fondation pour les études de défense nationale, 1980).

11. Andre Brigot, *Le désir d'Europe: L'introuvable défense commune* (Paris: Fondation pour les études de défense nationale, 1980).

12. See Wilfrid Kohl, *French Nuclear Diplomacy* (Princeton, N.J.: Princeton University Press, 1971).

13. See the contributions of the European authors in Lawrence S. Hagen, ed., *The Crisis in Western Security* (London: Croom Helm, 1982), particularly the article by Philip Windsor, "On the Logic of Security and Arms Control in Europe."

14. See, for example, Interview with Ambassador Malcolm Toon, *U.S. News and World Report*, March 15, 1981; and George W. Ball, "The German Problem," *New York Times*, March 29, 1981.

15. Peter Brandt and Herbert Ammon, *Die Linke und die nationale Frage: Dokumente zur deutschen Einheit seit 1945* (Reinbek bei Hamburg: Rowohlt, 1978).

16. See "Ein zählebiger Mythos: Stalins note vom März, 1952," *Frankfurter Allgemeine Zeitung*, March 10, 1982.

17. Egon Bahr, *Was wirden aus den Deutschen?* (Reinbek bei Hamburg: Rowohlt, 1982).

18. Gunter Gaus, "Der Westen, Polen, und der Kreml," *Die Zeit*, January 22, 1982.

19. Hans Ulrich Wehler, "Wir brauchen keinen neuen deutschen Sonderweg," *Frankfurter Allgemeine Zeitung*, February 15, 1982; and Heinrich August Winkler, "Sind sie Deutschen Nationalisten?" *Die Zeit*, January 29, 1982.

20. Peter Bender, *Das Ende des ideologischen Zeitalters Die Europäisierung Europas* (Berlin: Severin und Seidler, 1981).

Discussion of Part 4

Wolfram Hanrieder

There are three major reasons why many Europeans are skeptical about the earnestness of the Reagan administration's commitment to arms control. These reasons stem less than some people think from the occasional emotionalism of the peace movement in Western Europe; they are based on an appreciation of realpolitik and the imperatives of the military-strategic and political balance of power.

Briefly, the reasons are these: first, the realization that the United States has, in the postwar period, consistently followed a status quo policy toward Europe; second, the ambiguities and contradictions that are attached to U.S. linkage politics; and third, and specifically on arms control, the apparent self-interest of the United States in not following through with the double-track decision of December 1979, but making it a one-track decision that moves toward the planned deployment of modernized Pershing and cruise missiles in Western Europe.

Regarding the first reason, there is a realization in Western Europe—specifically in the Federal Republic of Germany—that the results of the détente of the 1970s have benefited primarily the Germans, not the Soviet Union and the United States. Many West Europeans expect, therefore, that any U.S. government, especially one with the ideological configuration of the Reagan administration, would take a second look at the prospects of détente in the 1980s, including those features that are focused on arms control. Skepticism in Europe about the prospects of arms control is thus connected with skepticism about U.S. willingness to deal with the challenges of a new European order. The view is widespread that both the United States and the Soviet Union prefer the European status quo, and that they tend to use their superior military-strategic position to compensate for diplomatic and economic infirmities.

The U.S. propensity toward linkage politics, as in Afghanistan and Poland, is also troublesome for many West Europeans. As practiced by the Reagan and Carter administrations, linkage politics connected with arms control measures is a sign of both U.S. weakness and U.S. strength. It is perceived as a sign of weakness because a truly hegemonic superpower does not need to engage in quid pro quo arrangements with its opponent: The United States would not have to bargain for good behavior on the part of the Soviet Union in Africa or in Latin America if it were sufficiently strong to implement its policies on its own. On the other hand, linkage politics, when attached to arms control measures, appears as a sign of U.S. strength: There emerges the constant implication that somehow arms control is more important to the Soviet Union than to the United States, otherwise why would the United States raise obstacles to the speedy and effective conclusion of arms control arrangements. Accurate or not, this is an image of U.S. arms control policy that emerges in Europe.

The third reason why Western Europeans are skeptical of the attitudes of the Reagan administration on arms control is that the deployment of modernized theater nuclear forces appears to be highly advantageous to the United States and that, therefore, the United States will insist on high Soviet payoffs if it were to forego that advantage. First, because of geographic factors, the Soviet Union cannot match the U.S. threat to the Western part of the Soviet Union by deploying intermediate-range nuclear systems of its own that could reach part of the United States— unless the Soviet Union would want to risk another Cuban missile crisis. Second, there is an incentive for the United States to deploy modern INF systems in Europe because of the weakening of the land-based leg of the U.S. triad of deterrence. The MX, seen by both Carter and Reagan as an effort to modernize the aging Minuteman systems, has so many technological, strategic, and political weaknesses that any solution for basing the MX is bound to be second-best and, moreover, can in no case be implemented until the late 1980s. Therefore, so many Europeans argue, there must be a great temptation for the Pentagon to use the deployment of modernized Pershings in Western Europe as an interim and substitute solution while it proceeds with the modernization of intercontinental systems based in this country. If the modernized INFs are emplaced in Western Europe by 1984, they would fill the interim gap that exists until the late 1980s, at which time the MX (as well as the Trident II) would be operative.

Catherine McArdle Kelleher

Our crisis-management system in Europe has functioned relatively well since the last major East-West conflict, the Berlin crisis in 1961. Yet at the same time, there is general belief, on both sides of the Atlantic, in the imminence of nuclear war. Public opinion figures have gone up startlingly regarding the expectation of nuclear war in the next ten years, one indication of general pessimism. In Europe, between 30 and 50 percent of those responding say that they expect nuclear war to occur within the next ten years. On this side of the Atlantic, the figures are between 15 and 22 percent, not enormously high but considerably higher than they were five years ago, or certainly ten years ago.

It is difficult to believe that this set of fears and anxieties is simply the effect of changes in structural-military posture on either side. At a very crude level of analysis, it is difficult to see from a popular view what difference the SS-20 makes compared to the city-busting potential the SS-4s and SS-5s have always had for European cities. Certainly, the Soviet buildup and the number of changes in readiness and force fill-out cannot be denied, but that is not the principal motivation for this basic level of anxiety and fear.

We are not dealing simply with a set of pacifist or neutralist notions. The general phenomenon of anxiety and concern must be fitted within what others have described as the crisis of governability. That is particularly true of continental European states at the moment. In many ways, we are seeing the details of defense policy choices that have been made quietly and without much attention over the last twenty years. Along this line, it is interesting that the Von Weiszäcker study done over ten years ago has only reached major popular consciousness (let alone a circulation outside of a relatively small expert community) in the last eighteen months in Germany, despite the fact that in the early 1970s it made dramatic predictions as to the small number of Germans who would survive even a limited nuclear exchange.

Generally, West European governments have found it easier to make choices without raising issues for public debates—the December 1979 double-track decision being an example—and who are now similarly less willing to take direct and public responsibility for the choices they have made. With the possible exception of Margaret Thatcher, most European political leaders face challenges within their own parties or within the coalitions that they lead, which can break down on single issues or on a set of economic factors. It is a situation in which hard choices and difficult programs, as well as basic issues of national defense, are simply postponed or left to public hand-wringing in the face of severe public questioning.

Another factor that has received considerable attention in the research community is the impact of demographic profiles in Western European countries. In a sense, Western European countries, because of birthrates during the 1950s, are currently going through a successor-generation crisis not unlike that experienced during the 1970s in the United States. There is an insistence that the debates that went on in the United States in the 1950s, and particularly in Germany in the late 1950s and early 1960s, must be reopened and the issues raised again. Members of the successor generation have as their benchmark what they perceive as the "normal" times of the early 1970s, and it is against that experience that they judge the actions and crises of the world in which they now find themselves. In many senses, this is a generation looking for leadership, while grappling with many of the same issues for which we thought answers had been already found.

A great deal of public debate and discussion is going on now, at a time not only of economic difficulty but at a time when economic reality of political and military choices is more observable to the individual citizen than it has been since perhaps the mid-1960s. One is struck by the situation in Germany, less in France, but certainly in England, where even supporters of national security spending are seeing the costs escalate beyond bounds. The hard choices that already exist within defense are complicated by even harder choices in terms of balancing defense requirements and social welfare requirements.

It is a situation that, if one were to approach it with the rational economist's eye, would call for the maximization across a broader base and the kind of specialization of force development that has been discussed fruitlessly in NATO almost from its inception. There are a number of unilateral arms reductions that will take place as certain types of functions and certain levels of forces become incompatible with the projected levels of growth and productivity that the major European states face over the next five years.

There are two central dimensions concerning arms control that will evolve in the 1980s. The first is the decision to be made about the continued role of the United States in the European security system. Clearly, the parallel question about the Soviet Union is important, but not to be discussed at the same level or subject to the same kinds of pressures. Is it conceivable that in 1990, as in 1980, 1970, 1960, and 1950, we can expect the "hostage" deposit of 300,000 U.S. forces in the European framework? Is their continued presence possible either in terms of acceptability to successive U.S. Congresses or to new leadership emerging in each NATO country? Are such forces even desirable, and if not, what kind of contribution will the United States make in an era of strategic stalemate, increasing doubt about the use of nuclear weapons, and the growing expense of conventional forces?

Second, the crisis management system and the alliance system in general has controlled the expansion and role of Germany and its potential for disturbing the European balance, as well as the East-West balance. What particular role is now to be assigned if Germany does not have the conventional Gaullist solution of the national nuclear force?

Precisely what kinds of responsibilities will be assigned now to a Germany far less willing, not to mention politically able, to endure the kinds of restrictions imposed on its rearmament almost thirty years ago?

Whatever system for crisis management is devised, these two central questions must be answered. They are not new questions, but that will not make them any less difficult to answer in the years ahead.

Joseph Kraft

The impressive evidence Jerry Hough has collected about the ongoing debate on basic priorities in the Soviet Union must be viewed with a certain skepticism. First, the general quality of the evidence is poor, coming as it does from people who are three or four levels down— journalists, professors, former officials. We know so little about how decisions are made in the Soviet Union, and it is hard indeed to draw any kind of conclusion from such soft evidence.

Second, the possibility that the Soviet Union is apt to go the Hungarian route seems extremely unlikely, if only because of the enormous importance of the Soviet military-industrial establishment. It is impressive to hear that Defense Minister Ustinov, on the one hand, is saying don't follow the Americans in an arms race, it's just a trap, and General Ogarkov, on the other, is saying we've got to do much more than we're doing and we've got to be tougher. It shows which way the tilt lies in the Soviet Union because it seems unlikely that General Ogarkov will be completely overwhelmed in that debate and also unlikely that the Soviet Union will go in any way that one could reasonably call the direction of a Hungarian model.

Third, the essence of politics is often not choice; the essence of politics is often the avoidance of choice. Soviet leaders are able to rationalize and harmonize seemingly impossible internal contradictions and pressures. The most likely outcome of any future leadership—of any succession—is another regime that will try to rationalize these conflicting pressures and that, far from making choices, will continue down the same path of avoiding them.

Washington has reacted and perhaps overreacted in dealing with what Jean Klein calls the German problem. It is cold comfort for Washington to be told that, after all, the German position had a French precedent and was implicit in studies made by the Max Planck Institute. That only indicates that the basic footing of policy with respect to European defense and the use of nuclear weapons there is unsteady. Furthermore, from a Washington point of view, what is going on in Germany looks significantly different from anything that has occurred before—in part, because of surrounding circumstances such as the following.

The fact is that you can have one Gaullist option, but if you have two or three, then the Western Alliance falls apart. There can be no imitation of the Gaullist move by the Germans. But if the Germans are slipping and uneasy, it is in a much different climate than back in 1958 when General de Gaulle voiced his suspicions and questions. At that time, we were still rather tight with the British. Now, with Britain turning inward, Germany is absolutely critical to the alliance, more than any other European country previously.

In addition, there was a feeling in Washington, based perhaps on unavowed self-doubts, that what was happening in Germany had a certain sympathetic harmony with things happening all over the world, with a movement that is well-founded, spreading, enduring, important— a shaping factor in U.S. politics of the future. But what will the outcome be? Will it have a benign effect? Will it cause our people in power to take notice and shape their policies accordingly? Or will they turn against this movement and try to organize a vigorous, nationalist, populist, patriotic reaction, as the Nixon administration successfully did against the Vietnam peace movement? People who look back on the Vietnam movement with such a rosy attitude have forgotten what happened in 1972. The fact is that the movement was by and large a failure, that it was revived posthumously thanks to Watergate. It is easy to organize against movements that take place on campuses and among intellectuals and that have strong counterreactions in the media.

It can be pointed out in conclusion that some of the comments here have reflected a feeling of being left out, a sense that it's us against them, a sense that the people who have concern about nuclear weapons are not part of the process. It is truly incumbent upon us to speak in ways that are not excessive, that are disciplined and discriminating, that reveal our real feelings, that are not self-indulgent, that are not designed just to command attention, but that are statements made by people who are part of the dialogue and part of a dialogue in which all of us have a stake.

Morton Schwartz

First, the good news. Professor Hough, as always, is imaginative and provocative in his analysis of Soviet affairs. Though without the same firmness of grasp on foreign policy as he has shown over the years in his writings on the Soviet domestic scene, this discussion of Soviet strategic perceptions is often quite gifted. His emphasis on the influence of the generational factor on Soviet thinking, for example, is striking and offers a persuasive explanation for the extraordinary continuity to be found in Soviet policymaking. The evidence on this score is breathtaking. The fact that 1983 was the first session of the UN General Assembly that Andrei Gromyko missed in over twenty years is a record that no other foreign minister could—or, I suspect, would want to—match. Along the same line, since he became foreign minister in 1957, Gromyko has faced across the negotiating table no less than nine U.S. secretaries of state and dealt with seven different presidential administrations. This longevity in office helps explain Moscow's exasperation with what they often see as the incessant shifts in the course of U.S. foreign policy—an exasperation, to be fair, also expressed by others. And Hough's judgment (articulated more fully in his original conference paper) that impending generational changes in the Soviet leadership offer the promise—I would say possibility—of policy changes is indeed worth careful attention.

Now, the bad news. Professor Hough's main point on the impact of what he views as the "changed strategic environment" on the thinking of the Soviet leadership is, in my view, very much off the mark. Though the Kremlin no longer should have as much to fear from more powerful foreign enemies as did Stalin—Hough rightly points out that peace has in effect been made with Germany, that China is no security threat, that the Soviet military's penchant for secrecy is counterproductive—Moscow's "irrationality" on these issues shows no sign of relenting. In Professor Hough's view, the Soviets have "no reason" to fear an attack from Western Europe or from China. The Kremlin leaders, from all the available evidence, calculate threats to their security rather differently.

Here we have a real paradox, one that is perhaps best explained by historians or cultural anthropologists. Although Moscow is militarily and politically more powerful than ever before, its behavior—toward its neighbors, toward other foreign powers, not to mention its behavior toward its own citizens—bespeaks a degree of neurotic insecurity and irrational fear that rivals even Stalin's. However more sophisticated the specialists associated with Andropov, their influence (as seen in recent events in Poland and Afghanistan, in the shooting down of the Korean airliner, and in the intensified repression of the tiny remnant of Soviet dissidents) is at best marginal. The much-promised reforms, the more moderate foreign-policy stance that they—and Andropov—were said to herald, show no sign of taking hold. However irrational and counterproductive in Hough's view, the Kremlin leadership seems persuaded that the "much-needed, long-overdue" economic reforms and "adaptations to strategic realities" are simply not relevant to their concerns.

Part 5

The Alternative to Arms Control

9

The Alternative to Arms Control

Barbara W. Tuchman

While anyone in his right mind is in favor of nuclear disarmament, many of us are skeptical of the capacity and willingness of governments to achieve it in any fundamental measure. Our skepticism is based on the history of disarmament in our century—a long, painful, repeatedly frustrated, always futile effort.

Disarmament is "a mirage and a will-o'-the-wisp," concluded Salvador de Madariaga of Spain, chairman of the League of Nations Disarmament Commission and Disarmament Conference.[1] No person has ever been better qualified to judge. Persistent failure of an endeavor, however, should cause it to be reexamined, not continued forever in the same manner. Another way must be found to prevent nuclear war, not necessarily ruling out disarmament but laying a new foundation for nonbelligerent coexistence. Now may be the time to seek it out because a new element has entered the situation—an impelling fear.

What follows will not be a discussion of weapons and strategies or an analysis of coupling and decoupling, windows of vulnerability, launch-on-warning, first strikes, theater deployment or any other of the nuclear esoterica. Nor will it be a discussion of the apocalyptic consequences of nuclear use—the deaths, devastation, radiation, and destruction of the human home, of which most people are fully aware.

A major predicament of the subject of nuclear arms control is that it is virtually incomprehensible to the layman. The layman finds it impossible to grasp the verifiable facts and potentials of nuclear weaponry because experts on both sides of the argument—the argument, that is, between advocates of more arms and advocates of disarming—give diametrically different statements of facts, or what they say is fact. One

---

Subsequent to the conference, this chapter was published in the *New York Times Magazine*, April 18, 1982. Reprinted by permission of Russell and Volkening, Inc., for the author. © by Barbara Tuchman.

side says the Russians are ahead; the other, that we are ahead; one, that we must close the gap; the other that there is no gap; one, that they can hit us before we can hit them; the other, that the case is the reverse. The public reads that the number of U.S. warheads ranges from 9,000 to 30,000 and that a similar range of variation exists for the Soviets. Of course, the variation depends on what is being counted, but since that is almost never precisely indicated, one cannot draw useful conclusions. Perhaps it does not matter, because no belligerent will ever have a chance to launch 9,000 warheads, much less 30,000. The public has no way of checking any of these statements or of knowing the truth. Indeed, there may be no truth.

Unlike all other arms systems prior to actual use, nuclear missiles have never been tried out in maneuvers. Their explosive power has been tested but not their performance in battle or in the destruction of nations, which should make one wary of all the dogmas. If there is one thing more certain than any other, it is that wars develop in ways that are unpredictable. The Maginot Line failed totally to perform the function it was designed and maintained for. The *Luftwaffe* and V-2 rockets did not knock out Britain. In the case of Vietnamese supply lines and our B-52 bombers, the result was not what the Air Force promised or expected.

In nuclear war, once communications and cities are blasted, decision making could fall into chaos. How will the belligerents, appalled by what they have done, reach each other to stop firing? Missiles with live warheads are flown over the magnetic pole; will they operate with the accuracy they did when tested without warheads inside our own borders? What about the speculative phenomenon interestingly called "fratricide," meaning the effect of warhead explosions on fellow warheads targeted in the same direction? These are unpredictables already considered, which only means there will be many more no one has yet thought of. The area of unknowns should warn us against taking announced doctrines and strategic scenarios on faith.

At the other end of technology and strategy is the peace movement— the wish for peace, world government, brotherhood, and all those goals of goodwill that humanity craves and has never attained. One must be skeptical of peace. Peace has not figured among the notable achievements of mankind. It is the most talked of and least practiced of all social endeavors. Men—in this case the male gender, not the species—are always saying they hate war and war is hell and so forth, and have continued to engage in it lustily, aggressively, and ceaselessly since the beginning of recorded history and doubtless before. Historians estimate that society has spent more time fighting than in any other activity except agriculture. Sumerians, Babylonians, Assyrians, Egyptians and

Israelites, Greeks and Romans, Scythians, Carthaginians, Huns and Goths, Mongols and Turks, Celts and Saxons, Europeans and Americans, Chinese, Japanese, and Muslims have fought each other or among themselves or against some opponent at every stage of civilization. Peace is brief, as fragile and transitory as apple blossoms in spring. Moreover, because it engages deep feelings, it produces sentimentalizing and distance from realism.

Somewhere between the strategists and the peace movement, we must find an area for creative thinking. It may lie in control, the control of war. Of course, that is certainly no new idea, although its history has been negative. In the early Middle Ages, when war was constant and indeed the gentry's profession, the church made an attempt to restrict its havoc by means of the Truce of God. During the truce, fighting was to be suspended on saints' days, Sundays and Easter, and all noncombatants—clerks, peasants, merchants, artisans, and even livestock—were to be left unharmed by men of the sword. That was the theory; in practice, the truce was a sieve consisting mostly of loopholes.

The concept of "just" war—that is, war in response to a wrong by the other side—was another effort to restrain the impulse to war. It received a great deal of attention, largely because the claim of a just cause entitled the belligerent to unlimited loot with a free conscience, loot being the primary object of medieval war. Since, as we all know, one's own motives are always just, the just-war concept never deterred anyone from aggression. Curiously enough, it turned up not long ago in a protest by members of the Harvard Divinity School calling for a worldwide freeze on production of nuclear weapons. They stated that "while there may have been just wars in the past, the inability to place traditional constraints on nuclear war now makes any moral justification impossible." While that is admirable and true, the authors, had they been historians, would have known that so-called "traditional constraints" have never been more than a verbal screen.

The history of control belongs largely to our century, the Terrible Twentieth, whose unconfined violence has made the need so compelling. That history has included attempts at disarmament or limitation of arms, international arbitration, international organization in the form of the League of Nations and the United Nations with their covenants and sanctions and systems of collective security. Even a pact of renunciation of war was signed by all the nations that counted in 1928.

Major international efforts began with the first Hague Conference on disarmament in 1899, followed by a second Hague Conference in 1907. Forced into existence by public pressure arising from fear of the swelling armaments industry and by the efforts of several extraordinary individuals, the Hague Conferences were a response to the frightening dynamics of the machine age, which seemed to be rushing toward explosion. In the same years, Alfred Nobel proposed a peace prize to compensate, one supposes, for the dynamite he had made available. The summons to a world conference, issued by Czar Nicholas II, who was behind in the arms race, surpassed the wildest dreams of the friends of peace and sounded, as one Viennese newspaper commented, "like beautiful music over the whole earth." Once in the hands of the governments—for no government could decline the summons—and of their delegations of top-hatted diplomats and bemedaled military, the results were carefully tailored to distress no war departments. Nothing done at the Hague restrained the Balkan wars from breaking out or the explosion of World War I.

The battered nations that emerged from World War I made a serious effort toward world order in the establishment of the League of Nations and the Permanent Court of International Justice, and they made a specific commitment to disarmament in the covenant of the League. In Article 8 of the covenant, recognized by the signatories as fundamental, they argued that "the maintenance of peace requires the reduction of national armaments to the lowest point consistent with national safety." The council of the League was mandated to formulate a plan of arms reduction for members to consider and act upon. New undertakings to confirm and carry out this purpose were added by the Treaty of Locarno in 1925.

The Committee on Disarmament worked for the next eight years in the attempt to implement Article 8, but agreement on means and principles broke down over the question of how to assure security before disarmament. General security was recognized as a prerequisite to disarmament, and sanctions against an aggressor as essential to security, but no nation was prepared to trust in the system to the point of disarming.

Meanwhile, the Washington Naval Conference of 1922 actually achieved the single act of arms control of the time—not disarmament but a limitation of battleships by the United States, Great Britain, and Japan in the ratio of $5:5:3$, and an agreement on nonfortification of the Pacific islands. As the first such act by the great powers, it was a stunning event, supplemented by the Nine-Power Treaty guaranteeing the integrity of China. Regrettably, the soul was less handsome than the face. Because Japan furiously resented holding the short end of the $5:5:3$ ratio, the effect of the treaties was ultimately negative. Resentment fueled the rising Japanese militarism that led eventually to Pearl Harbor, and the guarantee of China's integrity that Japan signed did not halt its program of expansion in China by so much as half an hour.

The League's efforts continued with the Geneva Protocol of 1924 for the Pacific Settlement of Disputes. Intended to reaffirm and strengthen the covenant, it provided for compulsory arbitration and defined the aggressor as the nation that refused arbitration. As this made the parties nervous about sovereign rights, the protocol was stillborn.

Optimism revived the next year with the Locarno Treaties, which committed Germany and France to mutual guarantees of boundaries and committed Germany to pursue the course of arbitration in any disputes with Belgium, France, Poland, or Czechoslovakia. A euphoric "Locarno spirit" prevailed and bloomed in the forever memorable Kellogg-Briand Pact engaging its signatories in the renunciation of war. The pact gained almost immediate and universal adherence because—according to one textbook that was either consciously or unconsiously cynical— "the pact only involved renunciation of aggressive war and made no provision for sanctions." In short, it was empty. Nevertheless, the ceremonial signing in Paris was greeted by French Foreign Minister Aristide Briand with genuine emotion as marking "a new date in the history of mankind" and by Secretary of State Frank Kellogg's happy assurance, "We have made peace at last."

The London Naval Conference of 1930 proved unable to translate this spirit into actual disarmament. It registered some limitations on submarines and other tonnages, amiably softened by an escalator clause which allowed an increase over specified tonnage if the "national needs" of any signatory demanded it. The descent from euphoria was under way, and was underlined a year later by the event that began the era of aggression and appeasement—Japan's seizure of Manchuria.

In 1932, the League's efforts at arms control finally culminated in the major Disarmament Conference of fifty-nine nations at Geneva. It adjourned without result because Germany, disarmed by the Treaty of Versailles, was now admitted to the League and demanding equality, which in turn caused France to cling rigidly to the principle that security must precede disarmament. Later, at a reconvened session in 1933, Britain, France, Germany, and Italy signed a No Force Declaration pledging "not in any circumstances to attempt to resolve any present or future differences between them by resort to force." Although a fine promise, it persuaded no one to disarm. But let us not wax too cynical about the verbal promises. They reflect what we genuinely wish, and they keep the wish alive, even if performance fails. Humanity's eternal difficulty is that thought is never matched by practice.

Collective security now unraveled fast. When the League adopted the Lytton Report blaming Japan as politely as possible for the Manchurian seizure, Japan departed from Geneva and officially repudiated the naval agreements of 1922 and 1930. Germany left the League six months later, denounced in its turn the Versailles Treaty, and announced its own rearmament based on the failure of the other nations to disarm as provided by the Versailles Treaty and the League covenant. As soon as its armed forces were sufficiently revived, Germany repudiated the Locarno settlement with France, and German troops reoccupied the Rhineland. At the same time, Italy invaded Ethiopia in a challenge that the League powers failed to meet by sanctions. Collective security was moribund and Munich not far off.

After World War II, the nations returned to the search for a system of international control. Confronted by the atom bomb, the United Nations tried, through the International Atomic Energy Agency, to lasso the new beast of war, but all ropes fell short. The United Nations Disarmament Commission, earnestly plodding in the footsteps of its predecessor, worked for five years to formulate a system for the limitation and balanced reduction of armed forces and armaments, the elimination of major weapons of mass destruction, and the effective control of nuclear energy for peaceful purposes. It, too, adjourned in deadlock. In 1959, a revised commission of five Warsaw Pact and five NATO countries resumed the effort without success. In 1961, the General Assembly adopted a resolution declaring the use of nuclear weapons contrary to international law, to the United Nations Charter, and to the laws of humanity. Comment fails. Judging by the race in nuclear weapons since then, resolutions of the General Assembly lack something in authority.

We come to 1962, the year of the Cuban missile crisis, when, thirty years after the League's Disarmament Conference, the United Nations Disarmament Conference convened in Geneva over the graveyard of its ancestor, with the declared aim of general and complete disarmament. Seventeen nations—with the notable exception of France—attended under the presidency of the United States and the Soviet Union and adjourned in the usual impasse. Nevertheless, in the waters off Cuba, something had happened: The shock of the near miss propelled the governments of the two parties to a serious effort at control. Together with Great Britain, they signed the Limited Test Ban Treaty of 1963, renouncing nuclear tests above ground, to which a hundred other signatories later adhered. Hailed with solemn joy as a real advancement at last by the peace advocates who had worked so hard for it, the test ban at least reduced radiation in the atmosphere. That was a gain for the environment but not for disarmament. It reduced no arsenals; it simply drove the tests underground. More tests have since been carried out underground than were previously carried out above ground. The total since 1963 is 783. In 1980 alone there were 49, or the equivalent of 4 a month: 20 by the Soviet Union, 14 by the United States, 11 by France, 3 by England, and 1 by China.

The Nonproliferation Treaty, adopted by the General Assembly of the United Nations in 1968 and since ratified by 116 nations, is a similarly qualified accord. It was meant to limit the acquisition of nuclear weapons capability. Since the treaty, that capability has been admittedly acquired in India, probably acquired by Israel, with Pakistan and South Africa said to be close behind. Argentina, Brazil, and Iraq are said to be working hard on the development, with South Korea and Taiwan possessing some degree of the technology.

Meanwhile, the development of a defensive weapon, the ABM, threatened to upset—or, as the strategists say, destabilize—the system to the point of initiating a race to produce anti-antiballistic missiles. As détente was still warm or lukewarm, the superpowers were sufficiently perturbed to enter strategic arms limitation talks and succeeded in 1972 in reaching the agreement called SALT I, which actually accomplished some limitation. It included a restrictive antiballistic-missile treaty and a so-called interim agreement temporarily freezing launchers of ICBMs and submarine-launched missiles at existing levels.

The inexhaustible creativity of the weapons men, however, was not frozen, and they soon raised lethal powers to a new stage. As a result, talks were renewed toward a more comprehensive mutual restraint, but arms limitation travels on such reluctant feet that it took seven years of negotiations before a signed agreement was reached. By that time, relations had so deteriorated that SALT II never even reached a vote in the Senate.

It might be added that in 1972 a Biological Warfare Treaty, prohibiting the development, production, and stockpiling of toxins and bacteriological weapons, was signed by the United States, Britain, and the Soviet Union. It entered into force in 1975 with a provision that any such weapons then in possession of the parties must be destroyed or diverted to peaceful purposes within nine months. Yet substantial reports have circulated of a Soviet anthrax program that violated this treaty, while the active chemical warfare recently reported in Afghanistan, if true, violated the Geneva Treaty of 1925—ratified by the Soviet Union in 1928—that prohibits belligerent use of chemical weapons. Plainly, there is nothing governments sign that they will not break.

This long and dreary survey serves to show that control of war in the form of disarmament or limitation of arms has been a fruitless effort. Even the *Encyclopedia Britannica*, coming to that conclusion in its last edition, was shaken from its usual composure to the outspoken admission that the effort for disarmament in our time has been "spectacularly unsuccessful." This suggests that we should try another way. Control of nuclear war is too serious a matter to be left any longer to governments. They are not going to get it for us; in fact, they are the obstacle. As

President Eisenhower recognized in that often-quoted and very revealing remark, "People want peace so much that one of these days governments had better get out of the way and let them have it."

What then is to be done? What change can be expected in a process that has accomplished nothing in eighty years? A change is possible because a new factor, terrible as it may be, has intervened: It is the prospect of finality. Before the advent of nuclear power, war—however devastating and brutal—had limits of destruction. The Mongols may have left pyramids of skulls, and the Nazis the equivalent in their gas chambers, but capacity was not global. It is often supposed, and stated, that turning war against civilians is an introduction of our century, but this is not so. The medieval way to destroy an enemy was to destroy his resources by killing off as many as possible of his working class. The punitive massacre of a city's inhabitants and the looting and burning of civilian property were normal procedures. What our century has introduced is not new inhumanity but newly extended capacity for mass destruction and ruin of the human home.

Until now, the finality of the human race and its living space was not within the framework of expectation. Today it is, which gives the question of control an urgency it never had before. The new factor is fear. It is fear that has given rise to the antinuclear movement in Europe and to the remarkable change in this country from the recent indifference to the new deep and widespread concern reflected in citizens' committees, bulletins and pamphlets, church groups' petitions, demonstrations, and conferences. In November 1981, a U.S. senator, David Pryor, Democrat of Arkansas, stated the case in a few words: "People are petrified, to put it simply."

Fear may make the difference. Heretofore, we have ascribed war to human aggression, to what William James called "the rooted bellicosity of human nature." "A millenium of peace," he maintained, "would not breed the fighting instinct out of our bone and marrow." Maybe not, but fear might. It is the only motive power, I believe, that could compel us toward the control of war that all the efforts of the last eighty years have not secured. It is an instrument, moreover, in the hands of the public. Governments, of course, are made up of human beings who know fear no less than ordinary mortals. But the trouble with governments is that they are moved by too many other considerations. Policymakers become trapped in illusions of power, individual ambition and self-image, vested interests, ideologies, hopes of reelection. As a result, fear has no room to energize common sense. Governments, it may be concluded, cannot be looked to for genuine disarmament or meaningful arms control.

Let us acknowledge it: The U.S. and Soviet governments have no real desire to limit nuclear arms. They go on talking about it as they are talking now at Geneva—and this is useful up to a point because it keeps the dialogue going—but the *intention* behind the talks is questionable. Perhaps it is indicated on our side by the appointment, as chief delegate to the Geneva talks, of the high priest of the hard line, Paul Nitze. A rough equivalent would be putting Pope John Paul II in charge of abortion rights. Governments that distrust each other do not seriously intend to reduce their arsenals. That is understandable, but we should understand it and not expect much.

Governments, like the rest of us, know that in a conflict of nuclear powers there can be no hard dividing line between conventional and nuclear warfare: One will slide inevitably into the other as soon as the choice for one side becomes either escalation or surrender. And they know that nuclear war, once started, cannot be limited, because the side that is losing will employ whatever remains in its silos. Strategists nevertheless talk of limited war, but that may be to let them sleep at night—besides providing material for a large and growing profession. They plan scenarios, play deterrence, juggle the acronyms, calculate delivery accuracy and counterforce capability, expound preemptive strike versus worst case, and intricately occupy their minds and skills in a way they could not if they acknowledged that the operation must end in a big bang. While they keep busy, the obstacle to progress is that the superpowers have got themselves into such a bind of mutual suspicion that they cannot divest themselves of a single missile. That will take a revolutionary change of attitude.

The principle necessary for such a change was stated by de Madariaga. Summing up his experience as the general manager of disarmament, he wrote in his memoirs that the causes of quarrel must be eliminated first before disarmament can take place. "The trouble with disarmament," he wrote in 1937, "was (and still is) that the problem of war is tackled upside down and at the wrong end. Nations don't distrust each other because they are armed; they are armed because they distrust each other. And therefore to want disarmament before a minimum of common agreement on fundamentals is as absurd as to want people to go undressed in winter. Let the weather be warm, and people will discard their clothes readily and without committees to tell them how to undress."[2]

The metaphoric warm weather is a long way off, but "a minimum of common agreement on fundamentals" is the essence. That is going to have to be our almost impossible task. If the nuclear threat is to be taken as seriously as all the passionate words of the peace advocates plead, we have no choice but to implement the Madariaga theorem.

While the problem is deeper than politics, the first step may have to be recourse to Horace Greeley's slogan, "Turn the rascals out!" The Reagan administration is explicitly, and probably immovably, attached to a policy of bigger and better and more arms, not less. To quote the Republican national platform of 1980, the party's object is "to close the gaps with the Soviets and ultimately reach the position of military superiority that the American people demand." This is nonsense even more than is normal for an electoral platform. One cannot know whether the American people demand military superiority or not, but for now and the foreseeable future, military superiority is an illusion, and delusion. If there is a gap, how is it measured? How do we know when we have closed it? The advocates of increase say it is measured by relative expenditures, but you might as well judge a beauty contest by what the contestants spend at the hairdresser. Expenditure does not tell you the quality or effectiveness of what it buys or the combat efficiency or commitment of those who operate the weapons. Military superiority is not a tangible or a static thing that one can get or keep. If we got it, it might last a week.

For the sake of clutching at this cloud, the administration insists upon a defense expenditure that is ultimately counterproductive because the cost will gradually erode civilian support for the defense program. Creating an unmanageable deficit and adding $50 billion each year to the national debt is the greatest cause of the inflation that is wrecking the economy and the welfare of our society. Americans may not be the most rational of people, but eventually enough of them will put two and two together to demand a halt.

Probably the Soviet people do not exist in serenity either. A study made in 1981 by the International Communication Agency, formerly the U.S. Information Agency, reports that while the Russians apparently do not fear direct attack, they suffer their own kind of apprehension about the United States as a power that can overwhelm them by superior military technology. In the popular view, the United States is seen as capable of changing the military balance in its favor overnight by some technological miracle that will leave the Soviet Union far behind in the arms race. Soviet governing groups, according to the study, harbor doubts "about the competence, reliability and effectiveness of their own forces." The possibility of direct conflict with the United States is no longer "dismissed out of hand," as it was formerly, although the Chinese, rather than ourselves, are seen as "the enemy," and the sense of inevitable conflict with China is "pervasive." Add to this the absence of self-sufficiency in food, the running sore of Afghanistan, the shift in their own population toward a possible majority of non-Russian peoples, and a border of unreliable satellite nations, and the sum is reason enough for uneasiness.

The idea, however, that the Russians might at some desperate moment plunge into foreign war to drown their internal dangers seems unlikely. U.S. theory holds that they would like to dominate, not by war, but through their possession of superior forces, nuclear and conventional, and therefore we must deploy greater forces lest we be dominated. If Soviet conventional forces started to roll across Europe, we are told, NATO conventional forces could not successfully oppose them, and therefore we would have to resort to nuclear weapons, first tactical and then, inevitably, when the enemy replied in kind, intercontinental land-based or submarine-based missiles.

Given nuclear weapons and their consequences, one thing is clear: *There is no military solution* to the problem. The confrontation of their system and ours has, let us repeat, no military solution. One of the congressmen who went to El Salvador in February 1982 to investigate the situation recognized this in the microcosm of that struggle. "I don't think," Representative James K. Coyne, Republican of Pennsylvania, was quoted as saying, "we can develop a military solution." That was astute and, as Coyne's Law, could justifiably be extrapolated to cover the larger rivalry of the United States versus the Soviet Union. Whatever the strategists and militarists and present-danger propagandists have to say about warfighting, as they oddly like to call it, there is no war of nuclear powers now that can be won or could end short of extinction. Earl Mountbatten, citing his fifty years of military service, told the public shortly before he was killed in 1979 that "the nuclear arms race has no military purpose. Wars cannot be fought with nuclear weapons."

That they must have the weapons anyway is the position of the Soviet and U.S. governments. This policy can only be deactivated, I think, by public rejection. There can be no real progress toward arms control until public tolerance of existing policy ends. When public tolerance stops, piling up overkill must stop, because as Christoph Bertram, former director of the International Institute for Strategic Studies, recently acknowledged, "without acceptance by the public, there can be no sustainable policy." The European antinuclear movement has already shown that governments and parliaments respond to public pressure, if for no other reason than fear of losing the next election. The deepest emotion of any person in high office is desire to stay in. The public wish not to be obliterated and not to be despoiled by grotesque military spending and insane national debt must make itself effectively felt. Military needs must be brought into proportion with the other needs of society, social and cultural.

When control of arms becomes a goal of the mainstream, then it will prevail. The working instrument is votes. Every candidate for elective office each November should be asked to state for the record his position on the arms race. We cannot suppose that reason will suddenly take possession of the human race and that a majority of every community will see the light of common sense within the next six months. I am a historian, not a mystic. Nor am I a Maoist believer in the ultimate wisdom of the "people." "Your people," said Alexander Hamilton unkindly to Thomas Jefferson, "is nothing but a great beast," but even a beast may balk at the edge of an abyss.

Public demand should continue for a bilateral nuclear freeze, ratification of SALT II, a ban on all nuclear testing, and, above all, for a firm renunciation of first strike by an act of Congress. These are necessary both to inform the public and maintain the pressure. Dramatizing the issue is Ambassador George F. Kennan's proposal for a sweeping 50 percent bilateral reduction of all nuclear arms without further discussion, to be followed by a further reduction of two-thirds of what remained. This cuts through the rhetoric and notifies us all how serious is a serious man's estimate of the situation. Yet with all due respect to Ambassador Kennan, something else must happen first.

Let us go back to the Madariaga theorem: The source of hostility must be eliminated or mitigated before nations will give up their weapons. Most people would say that to eliminate hostility between communism and free enterprise is impossible. Although it may be very difficult, it is not more so than disarmament, which has eluded our efforts so far; therefore we might just as well try another way. If all the energies, skills, intelligence, and at least half the money we have put to the use of the arms program were employed instead in an effort to reach accommodation or modus vivendi—that is to say, a way of living, not dying—we might in fact find it.

This does not mean we have to be friends. Friendship between a representative government based on liberty of the individual and a totalitarian government based on submission of the individual to the state can never be natural. We are not on a common path; we do not have political methods and principles in common; we share only one common goal—survival.

As long ago as 1957, the late General Omar Bradley saw this as the path. He asked why "we do not make greater, more diligent, more imaginative use of reason and human intelligence in seeking an accord and a compromise which will make it possible for mankind to control the atom and banish it as an instrument of war. . . . It may be that the problems of accommodation in a world split by rival ideologies are more difficult than those with which we have struggled in the construction of ballistic missiles. But I believe that if we apply to these human problems the energy, creativity and perseverance we have devoted to science, even problems of accommodation will yield to reason."[3]

That is such a brave belief that one cannot resist quoting it, although one knows from the study of history that reason does not control human motivation. Still, there are measures we might try. One would be a more massive, more purposeful effort than may now be conducted to promote antinuclear sentiment and fear of their own policies among the people of the Soviet Union and satellite countries. We are always blaming the Russians for agitating the peace movement in Western Europe. Why should we not do the same behind the Iron Curtain? We could also try what might be called the stuffed-goose option—that is, providing them with all the grain and consumer goods they need in large enough quantities that they would become dependent on us and could not risk the domestic turbulence that would follow if they cut off the source of supply by war.

Mistrust has to be tackled, and that is the hardest task. Diplomats and journalists who have dealt with Soviet officials see small chance of breaking through the granite wall of their recalcitrance. Yet living as we do now under a cloud of imminent explosion is too expensive and too socially destructive. We must find the way to coexistence without violence. If Germans and French, after centuries of hostility and three major wars in the last hundred years, could do just that from sheer necessity, perhaps we could, too. This is easily said, but it is a deeper, more basic enterprise requiring more radical readjustment of national thinking than another round of balancing your missiles against my missiles. A start might be made if leaders came to power in Washington and Moscow at the same time who both really *wanted* accommodation. Only both publics can make that happen.

Notes

1. Salvador de Madariaga, *Morning Without Noon: Memoirs* (Farnborough, England: Saxon House, 1974), p. 70.

2. Ibid, p. 48.

3. Speech at St. Albans School, Washington, D.C., November 15, 1957.

Suggestions for Additional Reading

Allison, Graham. *Essence of Decision: Explaining the Cuban Missile Crisis.* Boston: Little, Brown & Co., 1971.

Aron, Raymond. *Peace and War: A Theory of International Relations.* New York: Praeger Publishers, 1966.

ACDA. *Arms Control and Disarmament Agreements: Texts and Histories of Negotiations.* Washington, D.C.: U.S. Arms Control and Disarmament Agency, 1982.

Betts, Richard. *Surprise Attack.* Washington, D.C.: Brookings Institution, 1982.

Betts, Richard, ed. *Cruise Missiles: Technology, Strategy, Politics.* Washington, D.C.: Brookings Institution, 1981.

Blainey, Geoffrey. *The Causes of War.* New York: Free Press, 1973.

Blechman, Barry, ed. *Rethinking the U.S. Strategic Posture.* Cambridge, Mass.: Ballinger Publishing Co., 1982.

Brodie, Bernard. *Strategy in the Missile Age.* Princeton, N.J.: Princeton University Press, 1959.

————. *War and Politics.* New York: Macmillan Publishing Co., 1973.

Brodie, Bernard, ed. *The Absolute Weapon.* New York: Harcourt Brace, 1946.

Brown, Harold. *Thinking About National Security: Defense and Foreign Policy in a Dangerous World.* Boulder, Colo.: Westview Press, 1983.

Burt, Richard, ed. *Arms Control and Defense Postures in the 1980s.* Boulder, Colo.: Westview Press, 1982.

Carr, E. H. *The Twenty Years Crisis: 1919–1939; An Introduction to the Study of International Relations.* London: Macmillan Publishing Co., 1939.

Clark, Ian. *Limited Nuclear War: Political Theory and War Conventions.* Princeton, N.J.: Princeton University Press, 1982.

Claude, Inis. *Power and International Relations.* New York: Random House, 1962.

Deutsch, Karl. *The Analysis of International Relations.* Englewood Cliffs, N.J.: Prentice-Hall, 1968.

Dunn, Lewis. *Controlling the Bomb: Nuclear Proliferation in the 1980s.* New Haven, Conn.: Yale University Press, 1982.

Fallows, James. *National Defense.* New York: Vintage Books, 1981.

Freedman, Lawrence. *Evolution of Nuclear Strategy.* Cambridge, Mass.: Ballinger Publishing Co., 1981.

George, Alexander, et al. *Managing U.S.-Soviet Rivalry: Problems of Crisis Prevention.* Boulder, Colo.: Westview Press, 1983.

George, Alexander, and Richard Smoke. *Deterrence in American Foreign Policy: Theory and Practice.* New York: Columbia University Press, 1974.

Gompert, David C., et al. *Nuclear Weapons and World Politics: Alternatives for the Future.* New York: McGraw-Hill, 1977.

Gray, J. Glenn. *The Warriors: Reflections of Men in Battle.* New York: Harper & Row, 1959.

Green, Philip. *Deadly Logic: The Theory of Nuclear Deterrence.* Columbus: Ohio State University Press, 1966.

Greenwood, Ted, Harold Feiveson, and Theodore Taylor, eds. *Nuclear Proliferation: Motivations, Capabilities, and Strategies.* New York: McGraw-Hill, 1977.

Hanrieder, Wolfram, ed. *Arms Control and Security: Current Issues.* Boulder, Colo.: Westview Press, 1979.

Harvard Nuclear Study Group. *Living With Nuclear Weapons.* Cambridge, Mass.: Harvard University Press, 1983.

Heckrotte, Warren, and George C. Smith, eds. *Arms Control in Transition: Proceedings of the Livermore Arms Control Conference.* Boulder, Colo.: Westview Press, 1983.

Herken, Gregg. *The Winning Weapon: The Atomic Bomb in the Cold War, 1945–1950.* New York: Random House, 1981.

Herz, John. *International Politics in the Atomic Age.* New York: Columbia University Press, 1959.

Huntington, Samuel. *The Strategic Imperative: New Policies for American Security.* Cambridge, Mass.: Ballinger Publishing Co., 1982.

Independent Commission on Disarmament and Security Issues. *Common Security: A Blueprint for Survival.* New York: Simon & Schuster, 1982.

Jervis, Robert. *Perception and Misperception in International Politics.* Princeton, N.J.: Princeton University Press, 1976.

Kahn, Herman. *On Thermonuclear War.* Princeton, N.J.: Princeton University Press, 1960.

————. *On Escalation: Metaphors and Scenarios.* New York: Praeger Publishers, 1965.

Kaplan, Morton. *System and Process in International Politics.* New York: John Wiley & Sons, 1957.

Karas, Thomas. *The New High Ground: Systems and Weapons of Space Age War*. New York: Simon & Schuster, 1983.

Katz, Arthur M. *Life After Nuclear War*. Cambridge, Mass.: Ballinger Publishing Co., 1981.

Kelsen, Hans. *Principles of International Law*. New York: Holt, Rinehart & Winston, 1968.

Keohane, Robert, and Joseph Nye. *Power and Interdependence*. Boston: Little, Brown & Co., 1977.

Kennan, George. *The Nuclear Delusion: Soviet-American Relations in the Atomic Age*. New York: Pantheon Books, 1982.

Kissinger, Henry. *Nuclear Weapons and Foreign Policy*. New York: Harper & Row, 1957.

Lifton, Robert Jay, and Richard Falk. *Indefensible Weapons*. New York: Basic Books, 1982.

Meyer, Stephen. *Nuclear Proliferation*. Chicago: University of Chicago Press, forthcoming.

Morgenthau, Hans. *Politics Among Nations: The Search for Power and Peace*. New York: Alfred A. Knopf, 1948.

————. *Politics Among Nations: The Search for Power and Peace*. 5th ed., rev. New York: Alfred A. Knopf, 1978.

Olive, Marsha McGraw, and Jeffrey Porro. *Nuclear Weapons in Europe*. Lexington, Mass.: Lexington Books, 1983.

Platt, Alan, and Lawrence D. Weiler, eds. *Congress and Arms Control*. Boulder, Colo.: Westview Press, 1978.

Potter, William. *Nuclear Power and Nonproliferation: An Interdisciplinary Perspective*. Cambridge, Mass.: Oelgeschlager, Gunn & Hain, 1982.

Quester, George. *Nuclear Diplomacy*. New York: Dunellen, 1971.

Quester, George, ed. *Nuclear Proliferation: Breaking the Chain*. Madison: University of Wisconsin Press, 1981.

Rapoport, Anatol. *Fights, Games, and Debates*. New York: Basic Books, 1960.

Richardson, Lewis F. *Arms and Insecurity*. Pittsburgh: Boxwood Press, 1960.

————. *Statistics of Deadly Quarrels*. Pittsburgh: Boxwood Press, 1960.

Rosecrance, Richard, ed. *The Dispersion of Nuclear Weapons*. New York: Columbia University Press, 1964.

Rosenau, James, ed. *International Politics and Foreign Policy, Revised*. New York: Free Press, 1969.

Rush, Kenneth, Brent Scowcroft, and Joseph J. Wolf. *Strengthening Deterrence: NATO and the Credibility of Western Defense in the 1980s*. Cambridge, Mass.: Ballinger Publishing Co., 1982.

Schell, Jonathan. *The Fate of the Earth*. New York: Alfred A. Knopf, 1982.

Schelling, Thomas. *The Strategy of Conflict*. Cambridge, Mass.: Harvard University Press, 1960.

————. *Arms and Influence*. New Haven, Conn.: Yale University Press, 1966.

Singer, J. David, and Melvin Small. *The Correlates of War: I*. New York: Free Press, 1979.

Smoke, Richard. *War: Controlling Escalation*. Cambridge, Mass.: Harvard University Press, 1977.

Snyder, Glenn. *Deterrence and Defense: Toward a Theory of National Security*. Princeton, N.J.: Princeton University Press, 1961.

Snyder, Glenn, and Paul Diesing. *Conflict Among Nations: Bargaining, Decision-Making, and System Structure in International Crisis*. Princeton, N.J.: Princeton University Press, 1977.

Stockholm International Peace Research Institute. *Strategic Disarmament, Verification, and National Security*. London: Taylor & Francis, 1977.

————. *World Armaments and Disarmament: SIPRI Yearbook 1982*. London: Taylor & Francis, 1982.

Talbott, Strobe. *Endgame: The Inside Story of SALT II*. New York: Harper & Row, 1979.

Waltz, Kenneth. *Man, the State, and War*. New York: Columbia University Press, 1959.

————. *Theory of International Politics*. Reading, Mass.: Addison-Wesley, 1979.

Walzer, Michael. *Just and Unjust Wars*. New York: Basic Books, 1977.

Wolfers, Arnold. *Discord and Collaboration: Essays on International Politics*. Baltimore, Md.: Johns Hopkins University Press, 1962.

Wright, Quincy. *A Study of War*. 2 vols. Chicago: University of Chicago Press, 1942.

Yager, Joseph. *Nonproliferation and U.S. Foreign Policy*. Washington, D.C.: Brookings Institution, 1980.

York, Herbert. *Race to Oblivion*. New York: Simon & Schuster, 1970.

York, Herbert, ed. *Arms Control: Readings from Scientific American*. San Francisco: W. H. Freeman & Co., 1973.

Abbreviations

ABM	Anti-Ballistic Missile
ACDA	Arms Control and Disarmament Agency
ALCM	Air-Launched Cruise Missile
ASW	Anti-Submarine Warfare
B-1	Proposed replacement bomber for the U.S. B-52
C^3I	Command, Control, Communication, and Intelligence
CTB	Comprehensive Test Ban
ELF	Extra-Low Frequency
GLCM	Ground-Launched Cruise Missile
IAEA	International Atomic Energy Agency
ICBM	Intercontinental Ballistic Missile
INF	Intermediate Nuclear Forces
MAD	Mutual Assured Destruction
MBFR	Mutual Balanced Force Reduction
MIRV	Multiple Independently Targetable Reentry Vehicle
MX	Mobile Experimental Missile
NATO	North Atlantic Treaty Organization
PGM	Precision Guided Munition
SALT	Strategic Arms Limitation Talks
SIOP	Single Integrated Operational Plan
SLBM	Submarine-Launched Ballistic Missile
SLCM	Sea-Launched Cruise Missile
START	Strategic Arms Reduction Talks
UNSSOD	United Nations Special Session on Disarmament

For an elaboration of these terms and acronyms, see Wolfram F. Hanrieder and Larry V. Buel, *Words and Arms: A Dictionary of Security and Defense Terms* (Boulder, Colo.: Westview Press, 1979).

About the Contributors

Desmond Ball is a senior fellow in the Strategic and Defence Studies Centre at the Australian National University and a senior research associate with the Center for International and Strategic Affairs, University of California, Los Angeles.

Christoph Bertram, former director of the International Institute for Strategic Studies (1974–1982), is currently the foreign and political editor of *Die Zeit*, Hamburg.

Hans Bethe, 1967 Nobel Laureate in physics, is a professor of theoretical physics at Cornell University.

Richard Betts is a senior fellow in foreign policy at the Brookings Institution.

McGeorge Bundy, former National Security Affairs adviser to Presidents Kennedy and Johnson, is currently a professor of history at New York University.

Marvin L. Goldberger is the president of the California Institute of Technology.

Robert Grey is foreign affairs adviser to the Supreme Allied Command/Europe and former acting deputy director of the United States Arms Control and Disarmament Agency.

Wolfram Hanrieder is a professor of political science at the University of California, Santa Barbara.

Jerry F. Hough is a professor of political science at Duke University.

Neil Joeck is a research fellow at the Center for International and Strategic Affairs, University of California, Los Angeles.

Catherine McArdle Kelleher is a professor in the School of Public Affairs at the University of Maryland.

Donald M. Kerr is the director of the Los Alamos National Laboratory.

Jean Klein is a senior research associate at the Institut Français des Rélations Internationales, Paris.

Roman Kolkowicz is a professor of political science at the University of California, Los Angeles.

Joseph Kraft is a nationally syndicated American columnist.

Harold W. Lewis is a professor of physics at the University of California, Santa Barbara.

Michael May, a member of the U.S. SALT delegation from 1974 to 1976, is associate director at large for the Lawrence Livermore National Laboratory.

William Potter is a visiting associate professor of political science at the University of California, Los Angeles, and is the associate director of the Center for International and Strategic Affairs at UCLA.

Jack Ruina is a professor of electrical engineering at the Massachusetts Institute of Technology.

Morton Schwartz is with the Bureau of Intelligence and Research in the U.S. Department of State.

Charles Townes, Nobel Laureate for his role in the invention of the maser and the laser, is University Professor of Physics at the University of California, Berkeley.

Barbara W. Tuchman, twice a Pulitzer Prize winner, is an American writer and historian.

Kenneth Waltz is Ford Professor of Political Science at the University of California, Berkeley.

Charles Wolf, Jr., is dean of the Rand Graduate Institute at the Rand Corporation.

Herbert F. York, former U.S. ambassador to the Comprehensive Test Ban Negotiations, is currently the director of the University of California Institute on Global Conflict and Cooperation at the University of California, San Diego.

Other Titles in the Studies
in International and Strategic Affairs Series
of the Center for International and Strategic Affairs,
University of California, Los Angeles

William Potter, Editor, *Verification and SALT: The Challenge of Strategic Deception*, Westview Press, 1980.

Bennett Ramberg, *Destruction of Nuclear Energy Facilities in War: The Problem and the Implications*, Lexington Books, 1980.

Paul Jabber, *Not by War Alone: Security and Arms Control in the Middle East*, University of California Press, 1981.

Roman Kolkowicz and Andrzej Korbonski, Editors, *Soldiers, Peasants, and Bureaucrats: Civil-Military Relations in Communist and Modernizing Societies*, Allen & Unwin, 1982.

William Potter, *Nuclear Power and Nonproliferation: An Interdisciplinary Perspective*, Oelgeschlager, Gunn & Hain, 1982.

Steven L. Spiegel, Editor, *The Middle East and the Western Alliance*, Allen & Unwin, 1982.

R. D. Tschirgi, *The Politics of Indecision: Origins and Implications of American Involvement with the Palestine Problem*, Praeger, 1983.

Dagobert L. Brito, Michael D. Intriligator, and Adele E. Wick, Editors, *Strategies for Managing Nuclear Proliferation: Economic and Political Issues*, Lexington Books, 1983.

Raju G. C. Thomas, Editor, *The Great Power Triangle and Asian Security*, Lexington Books, 1983.

Jiri Valenta and William Potter, Editors, *Soviet Decisionmaking for National Security*, Allen & Unwin, to be published in 1984.

Bernard Brodie, Michael D. Intriligator, and Roman Kolkowicz, Editors, *National Security and International Stability*, Oelgeschlager, Gunn & Hain, to be published in 1984.

Index